WORD TRIPPERS

2nd Edition

Your **ULTIMATE SOURCE** for
Choosing the Perfect Word
When It **REALLY** Matters

Barbara McNichol

Word Trippers
2nd Edition

©2014 Barbara McNichol

www.WordTrippers.com

ISBN 978-1-939614-16-2

DEDICATION

Dedicated to the love of my life—first always—my husband, Byron.

Thanks for everything we share past, present, and future.

ACKNOWLEDGMENTS

I once edited a book for an author/expert who revised her acknowledgment pages so often by adding colleagues she cared about, her book never got published for fear of missing someone!

Because this word choice guide deserves to be in your hands sooner rather than later, I apologize if I've missed thanking key people who've traveled on this Word Tripper road with me.

Sincere thanks to these dedicated Word Tripper supporters: George Mason, Jenna Helgeson, Patrice Rhoades-Baum, Dan Poynter, Rhonda Scharf, Patricia Katz, Anita Paul, Faye Quam Heimerl, Karen Saunders, Claire O'Leary, Karen Reddick, Ronda Taylor, Rebecca Morgan, Ken Braly, Lynn VanLeeuven, Peggy Henrikson, Bob Kelly, and Jeff Rubin, founder of National Punctuation Day.

Overwhelming thanks to all subscribers of my Word Tripper of the Week ezine and the appreciative users of its variations along the way.

I'm honored by your praise and appreciation for my crusade to correct these pesky pairings that keep showing up in our language. A never-ending mission!

What Makes *WORD TRIPPERS* the Ultimate Source for Choosing the Perfect Word When It Really Matters?

The answer lies (not lays) on these pages. Use these alphabetized **WORD TRIPPERS** to guide you in choosing the perfect word.

What's the intent behind creating this word choice guide? So you will find it easy to make the right selection and avoid mistakes that fail to say what you want to convey.

With **WORD TRIPPERS** at your fingertips, you don't have any:

- Fat reference books to contend with
- Delays searching through dense dictionaries
- Emergency calls to former grammar teachers

This **WORD TRIPPERS** approach to choosing the perfect word has been discussed on radio talk shows, used in Wordshops, and featured in newsletters for authors, speakers, entrepreneurs, court reporters, administrative assistants, and many others.

Access (not assess) **WORD TRIPPERS** today.

It's the best way to actually find the perfect word when it really matters.

Enjoy words!

Ability, capability – "Ability" refers to skill while "capability" means aptitude. "After years of practice, he has the *ability* to play the piano. He also has the *capability* to learn more instruments."

Abstruse, obscure – "Abstruse" means difficult to comprehend for those with ordinary understanding. "Obscure" means deficient in light; far from centers of human population; out of sight, hidden, inconspicuous; vague or ambiguous. "The professor's lectures were so *abstruse* that students often felt lost, especially when he used *obscure* terms."

Accede, secede – Accede means to agree or assent; to give in to a request, to become a party to an agreement, treaty, office, or rank. Secede is to formally withdraw from an organization or alliance. "After much heartache and debate, the president *acceded* to the demands of the members who threatened to *secede* from the organization."

Acquiescent, quiescent – "Acquiescent" describes a person who is compliant and goes along without protest while "quiescent" characterizes a temporary state of inactivity. "After his operation, the patient was *acquiescent* in following the doctor's orders to remain *quiescent* at home."

Adept, proficient – "Adept" suggests an innate ability combined with a learned skill. "Proficient" describes ability that comes primarily from training and practice. "She encouraged her brother to become *proficient* at playing basketball, but he could never be as *adept* an athlete as she is."

Ado, adieu – "Ado" means bustle, fuss, trouble, while "adieu" expresses farewell. "There can be much *ado* about saying *adieu* when a loved one goes away."

Adopt, adapt – "Adopt" means to take as one's own (e.g., someone else's child), to choose (e.g., a lifestyle), or to formally accept (e.g., a position or principle). "Adapt" is to adjust to various conditions. "When you *adopt* a young girl, make it easy for her to *adapt* to your living environment."

Advice, advise – "Advice" is a noun; "advise" is a verb. "The *advice* you receive is only as good as the people who *advise* you." To remember the difference, think of the word "ice," which is a thing (a noun) and not an action (a verb).

Affect, effect – "Affect" is a verb meaning to change or influence. "Your quick action *affects* (influences) the outcome." "Affect" is also a noun to mean feeling, emotion, or emotional response. "During his grief process, my client displayed an uncharacteristically flat *affect*." "Effect" is a verb meaning to bring about, to cause. "You can *effect* (bring about) change easily." "Effect" is also a noun meaning result or outcome. "The story has a desired *effect*."

> **Pronunciation:** "Affect" as a verb has the accent on the second syllable (uh-FECT); "affect" as a noun places the accent on the first syllable (A-fect) with the "a" sounding like the vowel in "act." Using "effect" as a verb or noun, the accent is on the second syllable (eh-FECT or ee-FECT).

Affinity, infinity – An "affinity" is a natural attraction to something, a relationship by marriage, or an inherent likeness. "Infinity" refers to space, time, or quantity without bounds; an indefinitely large amount. "The *affinity* between the Air Force and NASA is evidenced by the number of astronauts who used to be pilots before leaving the skies for the *infinity* of space."

Affirm, confirm – "Affirm" means to declare positively or firmly, to assert as true or factual, while "confirm" means to verify, make firmer, strengthen, support or establish validity. "Working on the campaign helped *confirm* my intention to go into politics," he *affirmed* in his announcement speech.

Aisle, isle – An "aisle" is a passageway between rows of seats, shelving or columns. An "isle" is an island, especially a small one. "She walked the *aisles* of the bookstore until she found a calendar with photos of tropical *isles*."

Allay, ally – "Allay" means to relieve or reduce the intensity of something. "Ally" (as a verb) means to place in a friendly association or supportive role. "Ally" (as a noun) is a person in that association or role. "She can *allay* your fears by getting the president to *ally* with your cause and become an ally."

Alley, ally – An "alley" is a narrow passageway, walk, or back street between rows of buildings or in a garden; a lane or building for bowling. To "ally" is to form an alliance, association, or union with someone for a common purpose; an "ally" is the person or group with whom that connection is made; a plant or animal linked to another by genetic or evolutionary relationship. "Captain Heroic prowled the city's dark *alleys* with his superhero *allies*, saving innocents from evildoers."

Already, all ready – "Already" is an adverb meaning pre-viously or by this time, and refers to an action. "It's *already* too late to go." "All ready" is an adjective phrase meaning completely prepared. "She's *all ready* to go."

Alter, altar – "Alter" means to change or modify. "Altar" is a structure at which religious and sacrificial rites are performed. "The new deacon was asked to *alter* the *altar* at the church."

Alteration, altercation – An "alteration" is a change or modification to something, an adjustment. An "altercation" is a heated or angry dispute; noisy argument or quarrel. "The *altercation* between the two players created the need for an *alteration* in schedules."

Alternate, alternative – "Alternate" as a verb means to interchange repeatedly and regularly, or to do one thing after another in turn—e.g., to switch between walking and jogging. As an adjective, it means being in a constant state of succession or rotation. "When getting fit for sports, I *alternate* my daily workouts between lifting weights and running; this combination is the best *alternative* for me among a dozen possibilities."

Altogether, all together – The adverb "altogether" means entirely, completely, utterly. "That commute was *altogether* long and boring." The adjective phrase "all together" refers to a combination or group. "Those new factors taken *all together* reveal a different conclusion."

Allude, elude – To "allude" means to refer to casually or indirectly. To "elude" means to avoid or escape by cleverness or speed; to escape the comprehension of. "May the force be with you," the boy said to his friend, *alluding* to Star Wars, as they split up to better their chances of *eluding* the bully chasing them."

Ambiguous vs. ambivalent – "Ambiguous" means open to, or having several possible meanings or interpretations; equivocal. "Ambivalent" refers to conflicting thoughts or mixed feelings about someone or something; having difficulty choosing between two (or more) options. "I was *ambivalent* about the *ambiguous* answer I got to my question."

Amiable, amicable – "Amiable" refers to a person's pleasant, social, agreeable qualities; "amicable" describes something showing goodwill and friendliness. "The mediator's *amiable* personality helped bring about an *amicable* agreement."

Amity, amnesty – "Amity" means friendship and peaceful relations, especially among nations. "Amnesty" means a general pardon for offenses, especially political offenses. "Though the presidents of participating nations created an atmosphere of *amity* and trust at their meeting, they wouldn't all agree to grant *amnesty* to illegal residents."

Among, amongst – "Among" means surrounded by others (e.g., among friends) or in a group (e.g., among many things to do). Some dictionaries show "amongst" as an alternative to "among"; others don't even include it. "Among" is recommended because it's simpler and more contemporary than "amongst."

Among, between – "Among" occurs with MORE THAN two things or people; "between" happens with ONLY two things or people. "*Among* the 128 members, 92 have e-mail access. *Between* Gmail and Earthlink, Gmail is the more popular choice."

Amoral, immoral, nonmoral – "Amoral" doesn't involve questions of right or wrong, per se. It refers to someone having no moral standards, restraints, or principles; being unaware of or indifferent to what is right or wrong. "Immoral" means violating moral principles; not conforming to accepted patterns of conduct consistent with good personal and social ethics. "Nonmoral" is synonymous with "amoral." "In combat, soldiers must accept an *amoral* world; much of what they must do would be *immoral* in a peaceful society."

Anagram, acronym – An "anagram" is a word or sentence formed by rearranging the letters in another word or sentence. An "acronym" is a word formed from the initial letters of a name or series of words. The word "read" is an *anagram* of the word "dear." USA is an *acronym* for United States of America.

Anecdote, antidote – "Anecdote" is a short account of an incident, a mini-story. "Antidote" is a remedy to counteract the effects of a condition (e.g., poison, disease, etc.). "Telling an *anecdote* that's funny is an *antidote* for boredom."

Annuals, perennials – Plants that are "annuals" last for one growing season ("annual" pertains to one year) while "perennials" have a life cycle that lasts more than two years. "I like to plant a variety of *annuals* every spring, but I think more carefully when I choose *perennials* because they last longer."

Anonymous, unanimous – "Anonymous" means unknown originator. "Unanimous" means everyone sharing the same opinions or views. "The poem written by an *anonymous* contributor received *unanimous* approval from the magazine's editorial board to feature it next month."

Antagonist, protagonist – An "antagonist" is an adversary who competes against another; a "protagonist" is a chief proponent of a cause. In literature, the antagonist is the opponent of the protagonist, who is the hero or leading character. "If the *protagonist* has enough supporters on his side, the *antagonist* won't win the conflict."

Anyway, any way – The one-word version means "in any case" while the two-word version refers to possibilities. "Is there *any way* we can meet today? I'll make an appointment for 4 p.m. *anyway*." Note: never use "anyways."

Anxious, eager – "Eager" means exciting or enthusiastic. "Anxious" means full of anxiety or worry. "I'm *eager* to hear the details of your trip." "I have been *anxious* to learn about your travels ever since I heard about the airline strike."

Appear, seem – Use "appear" when it means to come forth and "seem" to indicate how someone probably looks like or feels. "Whenever that singer *appears* on stage, she *seems* happy."

Appraise, apprise – "Appraise" is to assess or determine the worth of something (e.g., a house, land) while "apprise" means to inform or alert someone to something significant. "The real estate agent *apprised* the owner of his house's *appraised* value."

Arcane, archaic – "Arcane" refers to knowledge that is secret, mysterious, and known by few. "Archaic" means characteristic of an earlier time, antiquated. "The ability to use a slide rule is an *arcane* skill; electronic calculators have completely replaced such *archaic* devices."

Arrant, errant – "Arrant" is an adjective meaning without moderation, extreme. It's synonymous with complete or consummate. "Errant" refers to straying from a proper course or standard. "He can be called an *arrant* fool for taking an *errant* route to spending his inheritance."

Artful, artistic – "Artful" means slyly crafty or cunning; exhibiting art or skill; skillful in adapting means to ends. "Artistic" means showing imagination and skill; concerning art or artists; exhibiting taste, sensitivity, or appreciation of art and beauty. "Technically skilled but unimaginative, the painter made a living doing *artful* reproductions of Renaissance masters rather than his own *artistic* creations."

Ascetic, aesthetic – An "ascetic" is a person who renounces the comforts of society to follow a life of self-discipline; a hermit. "Aesthetic" relates to appreciating beauty characterized by a love of beauty; concerned with pure emotion rather than pure intellectuality. "Just because the *ascetic* displayed nothing on the walls of his room doesn't mean he lacks *aesthetic* sensibility."

Assess, access – "Assess" is to determine the value, significance, or extent of. "Access" is the ability to approach, communicate with, or make use of. "First *assess* the damage, and then determine if the site is safe enough for public *access*."

Assume, presume – Both imply taking something for granted but "assume" means supposing something is true while "presume" shows a higher level of confidence. "I *assume* he'll arrive when he says he will." "Please don't *presume* you're always right."

Augur, auger – As a noun, an "augur" is a seer or prophet who foretells events by interpreting signs and omens. As a verb, "augur" means to divine or predict; to serve as an omen or promise of something. An "auger" is a hand tool used for boring holes in wood or ice. "The *augur* warned the ice fishermen about using a poorly made *auger* that wouldn't cut through the thick ice."

Autocrat, aristocrat – An "autocrat" is a ruler who has absolute power. An "aristocrat" has been born into the nobility or ruling class. "Although the *autocrat* yearns to be an *aristocrat*, he lacks the bearing that comes from a privileged upbringing."

Avenge, revenge – "Avenge" is used when there's a moral intention to right a wrong; "revenge" shows a desire to inflict punishment for an insult or injury. "They want to *avenge* injustice by taking *revenge* on those who hurt them."

Average, median – "Average" means between the extremes; usual or ordinary. "Median" means toward the middle. In statistics, it's the middle number of a group, with equal numbers above and below it. "While an *average* is reached by adding all factors and dividing by how many there are, the *median* is a slice through the middle."

Averse, adverse – "Averse" means having a strong feeling of opposition or repugnance. "Adverse" refers to unfavorable or antagonistic circumstances. "I am *averse* to putting myself in *adverse* weather conditions."

Avert, avoid, evade – "Avert" is to prevent or turn away from, to ward off. "Avoid" means to stay clear of, to keep away from, shun. "She *averted* her eyes when she came close to the car accident to *avoid* seeing people injured." "Evade" implies escape or elusion, often through trickery. "The contractor built the railing to *avoid* any accidents." "I stretched the truth to *evade* paying the traffic ticket."

Awhile, a while – "Awhile" means "for a while" (that is, for a period of time). Therefore, it's redundant to say "for awhile" because it's like saying "for for a while." "Let's get together *awhile*. We can drink and enjoy visiting *for a while*."

Bad, badly – Use "bad" with intransitive verbs (e.g., look, feel, sound, taste) and "badly" with all other verbs. "The soccer team looked *bad* because its members played *badly*."

Bear, bare – "Bear" as a verb means to carry, support, or hold in one's mind. "Bare" means to expose or uncover. "Instead of *bearing* a grudge against his neighbor, he cleared the air by *baring* his true feelings about the incident."

Bemuse, amuse – The verb "bemuse" means to bewilder or confuse (someone) while "amuse" refers to holding someone's attention pleasantly, in a cheerful manner. As adjectives, the forms are "bemused" and "amused/amusing." "I was *amused* by the *bemused* looks of those viewing the abstract art."

Benevolence, beneficence – "Benevolence" is the desire to do good to others, be kind, charitable. "Beneficence" is active goodness, kindness, or charity. Both words can refer to the kind act or gift itself, but in general, benevolence is *wanting to do good* and beneficence is *actually doing good*. "The employer's *benevolence* was demonstrated by his *beneficence* in giving all his employees holiday bonuses."

Bereaved, bereft – "Bereaved" means deprived by death while "bereft" refers to a general deprivation. "Bereft" is the archaic past participle of bereaved. "The *bereaved* widow also felt *bereft* of the hope she once had."

Better, best – "Better" is used to compare TWO items while "best" refers to one of MORE THAN TWO items. "It's *better* to schedule your workshop on a Tuesday than a Wednesday, but Thursday is the *best* day in the week for most people."

Bi, semi – "Bi" occurs every two intervals; "semi" occurs twice during a time period. "I publish a *bi-monthly* newsletter, sent every other month, rather than a *semi-monthly*, which goes out twice a month."

Birth, berth – "Birth" is the act of bearing offspring; the event of being born; the time when something begins; origin; lineage. "Berth" means a shelf-like sleeping space, as on a ship, airplane, or railroad car; sufficient space for a ship to maneuver; a space for a ship to dock or anchor; a job or position. "The sailor read a letter announcing the *birth* of his son while lying in his *berth* aboard his battleship."

Boarder, border – A "boarder" is a person who pays for lodging and often regular meals, someone who rides a board athletically (snowboard or surfboard), or is a member of a boarding party. A "border" is the outer boundary of a surface or area; the line separating geographic regions; an ornamental design around the edge of a picture, or a garden; to "border" is to form or be one. "Her *boarder* was low on cash, so she let him earn his keep by planting flowers along the *border* of the yard."

Bolder, boulder – "Bolder" means more bold, i.e., more fearless, daring, courageous or conspicuous. A "boulder" is a large, rounded rock. "The art instructor told her to use *bolder* colors in her paintings, not just pastels." "The *boulder* rolled down the hill after heavy rains loosened the dirt around it."

Boom, boon – As a noun, "boom" is a long pole extending from a mast, or a long, movable arm used to maneuver a microphone; it is also a loud noise. As a verb, it means to make a resonant sound or to progress rapidly. "Business is *booming*." "Boon" refers to a benefit, especially in response to a request. "Lower interest rates are a *boon* to homeowners."

Born, borne – "Born" means brought forth by birth, or possessing stated qualities from birth. "Borne" is a form of the verb "to bear," which means to hold up, transport, carry in the mind, yield; exhibit a quality or characteristic. "He was *born* lucky." "Pain from the loss of my child will be *borne* until I die."

Breath, breathe – "Breath" (a noun) means the air you inhale and exhale; "breathe" (a verb) is the action of taking breaths. "The jogger had to *breathe* hard until he could catch his *breath*."

Bridal, bridle – "Bridal" means of, for, or pertaining to a bride or a wedding. A "bridle" is a harness consisting of a headstall, bit, and reins that restrains and guides a horse; it can also mean to curb or restrain. "The *bridal* party waiting under the wedding canopy watched the groom arrive on a white steed with an ornate *bridle*."

Browse, peruse – "Browse" means to review something (usually, a written document) in a casual or leisurely way, while "peruse" calls for reading it thoroughly, examining it with care. "When we read the newspaper, we usually *browse* through the display ads but *peruse* the help-wanted section so we don't miss any job opportunities."

Cache, cachet – A "cache" (sounds like "cash") is a hiding place, especially one in the ground for ammunition, food, treasures, or anything hidden that way. "She hid her jewels in a *cache* behind the barn for safekeeping." As a verb, it means to hoard, stockpile, reserve, store. "She *cached* her money under her mattress." "Cachet" (rhymes with "sash-*ay*") is an official seal on a document, a distinguishing mark or stamp; a sign or expression of approval; superior status; prestige. "The document carried the *cachet* of the president's signature."

Caliber (calibre), caliper(s) – "Caliber" refers to the diameter of bullets or other projectiles as well as the inner diameter of a hollow cylinder (e.g., the barrel of a gun). It also means quality or degree of worth. "Parents want to enroll their children in schools of high *caliber*." "Calipers" are instruments that measure depth, thickness, or distance between two points. "Fitness trainers use *calipers* to measure body fat."

Canvas, canvass – "Canvas" is a kind of cloth; "canvass" means to solicit votes or sales; discuss thoroughly; ascertain through questioning. "Red Cross volunteers *canvassed* those giving blood before they went to the *canvas* tent to donate."

Capital, capitol – As an adjective, "capital" means primary or principal. "The subject is of *capital* concern." As a noun, "capital" refers to wealth, a city where government is located, and an uppercase letter. "Much of my *capital* is in stocks." "Ottawa is the *capital* of Canada." "Capitol" refers to the building that houses legislative sessions. "You will find the *capitol* building in the *capital*."

Capture, captivate – To "capture" means to take possession of by force or stratagem; to gain control or exert influence over; to record in lasting form (e.g., an event on film). "Captivate" means to get and hold someone's attention through charm, beauty, or excellence. "Enemy soldiers *captured* the king while the queen *captivated* the crowd with her singing."

Career, careen – "Career" as a noun refers to one's occupation or profession. "Career" as a verb means to go at full speed. "Careen" means to lean or tip to one's side while in motion. "While *careering* along the dark country road, the young driver *careened* into a snow bank and rolled his car."

Carrot, carat, karat – A "carrot" is an orange-colored vegetable. A "carat" is a unit of weight for precious stones equal to 200 milligrams while a "karat" measures the fineness of gold (e.g., a 12-karat gold piece is 50% pure gold). (Note: sometimes karat is spelled carat.) "On the scale of good nutrition, a *carrot* might be the equivalent of 24-*karat* gold." "The number of *carats* in the ruby exceeded the number of *karats* in its gold setting."

Cavalry, calvary – "Cavalry" refers to mounted soldiers or a highly mobile army unit using vehicular transport, such as light armor and helicopters. "Calvary" refers to either a sculpture representing the crucifixion or an experience of extreme suffering. "In one battle of the Franco-Prussian War, the French *cavalry* fought German infantry on a height by the *Calvary* of Illy."

Censor, censure – A "censor" is an official who examines literature, TV programs, movies, etc., for the purpose of documenting, rating, or deleting objectionable parts. It also means to act as a censor. "Censure" is a strong expression of disapproval, a reprimand. As a verb, it means to criticize in a harsh manner. "The official *censor* not only *censored* the scene in the film but also *censured* its director for including vulgar language."

Censure, censorious – "Censure" as a verb means to blame, disapprove, officially rebuke. As a noun, it means the expression of blame, disapproval, and rebuke. "Censorious" is an adjective describing a tendency to criticize or find fault. "The *censorious* school board issued yet another *censure* of the high school teacher's use of expletives in the classroom."

Cerebration, celebration – "Cerebration" is the act of thinking. "Celebration" is the observation of a day or event with ceremonies of respect, festivity, or rejoicing. "It took a great deal of *cerebration* to plan her husband's surprise 40th birthday *celebration*."

Ceremonial, ceremonious – "Ceremonial" describes something characterized by formality or ritual, or used with ceremonies. "Ceremonious" refers to those given to actions marked by ritual, elaborate etiquette, or politeness. "The priest took his *ceremonial* robe and, with a *ceremonious* sweep of his arm, draped it over his shoulders."

Childish, childlike – When adults are "childish" they behave immaturely or foolishly; when they're "childlike" they behave with the wonder, creativity, and innocence of a child. "Their complaints about the service sounded *childish*, given the overcrowded conditions at the restaurant." "The team's *childlike* approach to brainstorming gave us many creative ideas."

Chute, shoot – They are pronounced the same and their definitions overlap. However, "chute" refers to an inclined channel or vertical passage for conveying material to a lower level, or to move or deposit by means of such a channel. To "shoot" means to discharge a weapon, take a photograph or video, or perform a rapid movement; as a noun, a "shoot" is new plant growth. "The escaping convict hesitated before sliding down the coal *chute*, but he had little choice as the guards were *shooting* at him."

Clamber, clamor – "Clamber" is a verb meaning to climb something, often awkwardly, as when scrambling over obstacles. "Clamor" as a noun is a loud outcry or hubbub; as a verb, it means to protest, complain, or demand; shout loudly and insistently. "In their *clamber* up the boulder-strewn mountain trail, the lost hikers had to *clamor* for help."

Climactic, climatic – "Climactic" refers to a climax, which is an intense point or moment leading to an ending, while "climatic" refers to weather conditions. "The weather announcer predicted *climactic* results for people close to the center of the storm in his report on *climatic* changes."

Clinch, clench – "Clinch" is a variation of the older "clench," so their meanings partly overlap; both can be used as a noun or verb. "Clinch" means to settle something decisively (e.g., a dispute or contest); to secure or fasten (with or applied to a nail); to constrain by embracing (as combatants in a boxing match). "Clench" refers to closing tightly or grasping firmly (e.g., one's jaws or fist); to grip tightly with a tool. "After the quarterback made his game-*clinching* touchdown pass, he thrust his *clenched* fists into the air in a victory salute."

Colonel, kernel – A "colonel" is an officer in the armed forces or an honorary title in some southern states. A "kernel" is the inner, edible part of a seed, nut or fruit; the central part or core of something. "Supplies were running low so the *colonel* told his men to savor every crumb of bread and *kernel* of corn."

Collegial, congenial – "Collegial" means character- ized by having power and authority shared equally among colleagues; resembling or typical of a college or college students. "Congenial" means agreeable, suitable, or pleasing in nature or character; having the same tastes, habits, or temperament. "At his work, the office environment was *collegial* rather than hierarchical; if not for having to wear a necktie and work in a cubicle, he would have called his job *congenial*."

Comparative, comparable – "Comparative" means pertaining to comparison; using comparison as a method of study, e.g., comparative anatomy. "Comparable" means capable of being compared; similar or equivalent. "Although a *comparative* newcomer to the field, he still believed his achievements were *comparable* to those of the more experienced applicants."

Compel, impel – "Compel" means to force, drive, or constrain, especially to a course of action. "Impel" means to urge forward or incite; propel. "The servant was *compelled* to explore the dark cave because his master was *impelled* by curiosity to discover its secrets."

Comment, commentary – A "comment" is a brief statement of fact or opinion. "Commentary" is one or more statements (written or oral) containing opinions, explana- tions or interpretations. "The announcer's sarcastic *comment* about the team's losing streak punctuated his ongoing *commentary* about the players' poor skills." Also, "com- mentary" refers to anything that makes a point or provides a perspective. "The neighborhood's high crime rate is a sad *commentary* on failed social programs."

Compliment, complement – "Compliment" means to praise while "complement" means to complete or enhance something. (Note: the words "complete" and "complement" both use the letter "e") "The wine steward deserves many *compliments*. The wine *complements* the food extremely well."

Complimentary, complementary – When you use the "i" version, you are giving praise. When you use the "e" version, you are completing or enhancing something. (Memory trick: The word *complete* has an "e.") "The meeting planner was *complimentary* about my speech because it was *complementary* to other talks at the conference."

Comprise, compose – "Comprise" refers to the whole that has a number of parts while "compose" refers to the parts making up a whole. It's correct to say, "The book is *composed* (made up) of four short stories." It's incorrect to say, "The book is comprised of 22 chapters." Instead, say, "The book *comprises* (consists of) 22 chapters."

Connote, denote – "Connote" means to suggest or imply meanings or ideas in addition to the literal meaning; to have as a related or attendant condition. "Denote" means to be a name or designation for; to mark or indicate. "The phrase 'amber waves of grain' is more often used to *connote* America's abundance than to *denote* an actual field of wheat."

Conscious, conscientious – "Conscious" is to be aware of something; "conscientious" is to be diligent in performing a task. "After the previous manager didn't work out, the owner became more *conscious* of hiring someone who was *conscientious*."

Contemporary, contemporaneous – While both adjectives mean occurring at the same time, "contemporary" usually refers to people and things while "contemporaneous" refers to events and facts. "History shows examples of one person being the *contemporaneous* ruler of two countries, an unlikely occurrence in *contemporary* times."

Content, context – "Content" means something that's contained; the subject matter. "Context" is the surrounding words, the atmosphere or background, or a set of facts or circumstances that lend meaning to something. "Although the *content* of the ancient scientific work is interesting, when put in historical *context*, amazing insights emerge."

Continual, continuous, contiguous – "Continual" means recurring frequently; "continuous" means without interruption. "Contiguous" means bordering, adjoining, abutting, adjacent. "It's been a *continual* push to keep my business moving." "The river flows *continuously* in the spring." "In the U.S., the term 'contiguous states' excludes Hawaii and Alaska because their borders don't touch other states."

Convince, persuade – You "convince" someone of an idea but "persuade" someone to take action. Therefore, it's correct to say, "He *convinced* me it would taste good" but incorrect to say, "He convinced me to taste it." Instead, say, "He *persuaded* me to taste it."

Corn, kernel – "Corn" refers to the edible seeds of the corn plant and to the plant itself as well as to grains in general. "Kernel" applies to the seed or, technically, the inner part of a seed or similar plant part. It also denotes an essential component of a concept. "When making popcorn, it's the *kernel* of the corn that actually pops, not the *corn* itself."

Corroborate, collaborate – "Corroborate" means to strengthen or make more certain with other evidence. "Collaborate" means to work together, especially in a joint intellectual effort. "It's common for the defense lawyers working on a court case to *collaborate* with each other while they *corroborate* the evidence being gathered."

Counsel, council – "Counsel" as a verb means to give advice. As a noun, it means a lawyer or professional who gives advice. "Council" is a group of people who acts on stated matters. "The *council* will ask for legal *counsel* to advise the new people coming to town."

Course, coarse – As a noun, "course" means a direction or route, path, or channel along which anything moves. "He ran on a course that went through the forest." As a verb, it means to go along a path or channel, to move swiftly. "Anger *courses* through his veins." Its homonym "coarse" is an adjective meaning rough-textured or characterized by large particles (a *coarse*, sandy beach) or lacking in fineness or delicacy (a *coarse* way of speaking). The noun form is coarseness. "The metal file had a high grade of *coarseness*."

Criticism, critique, review – A "criticism" is an evaluation or judgment of something, while a "critique" is an elevated term for the same thing. A "review" is used as a synonym for these but may also imply a more comprehensive study. (Roget's New Millennium™ Thesaurus, First Edition, v 1.3.1)

Current, currant – A "current" is a steady flow or directional movement, especially of air, water, or electric charge, or the rate of such movement; as an adjective, it means of the immediate present, in general circulation, or common knowledge. A "currant" is a small, dried seedless grape from shrubs of the genus Ribes. "To test the river's *current*, she tossed a piece of her *currant* bun into the water."

Cymbal, symbol – A "cymbal" is a round piece of metal used as a percussion instrument. A "symbol" is something that stands for something, especially a material object that represents something intangible. "A crescendo of *cymbals* from the orchestra signaled the unveiling of the statue of a bald eagle, long recognized as the *symbol* of U.S. strength and independence."

Dabble, dapple – "Dabble" means to do something playfully or superficially, or to splash with liquid. "Dapple" is a mottled or spotted marking. "She *dabbled* at *dappling* the walls with paint."

Decedent, descendant – A "decedent" is a legal term for dead person while a "descendant" is a blood relative of a later generation. "The estate of the *decedent* has never been probated." "My neighbor is a *descendant* of a famous general."

Deference, difference – "Deference" means submission or courteous respect. "Difference" is being unlike or dissimilar. "He discontinued his argument in *deference* to their *difference* of opinion."

Deification, reification – "In the unlikely event that you're ever offered the choice between *deification* and *reification*, it's probably wise to go with the former, which is the condition of being treated as a god, rather than the latter, which is the condition of being treated as a thing." - from Visual Thesaurus

Delegate, relegate – "Delegate" means to send another as one's representative; to commit or entrust to another. "She *delegates* her assistant to represent her at the meeting." Relegate carries a connotation of status and means to consign to an inferior position, place, or condition. "He *relegates* the less pleasant tasks to his assistant."

Demure, demur – "Demure" as an adjective means to be modest, shy, or reserved in manner. To "demur" as a verb is to voice opposition, to delay decision or action while, as a noun, "demur" is an objection or delay. "In her *demure* way, the young parent stood up at the meeting and *demurred* at the motion to implement a new school policy. Many others supported her *demur*."

Deprecate, depreciate – "Deprecate" is to heap with scorn; to belittle. "Depreciate" is to lessen in price or value. "To cover his insecurity, he would *deprecate* his coworkers by telling untrue stories about them." "A new car *depreciates* (loses its value) as soon as a buyer drives it off the dealer's lot."

Deprived, depraved – "Deprived" characterizes the lack of something desired or valued, a necessity of life such as food or shelter. "Deprived" also describes a disadvantaged socio-economic class or condition. "Depraved" means corrupt, wicked, or perverted. "The *depraved* thief said his actions were the result of his *deprived* childhood."

Descent, dissent – "Descent" is a slope; a downward incline or passage; a decline in status or level; the act of going down. "Dissent" as a noun is a difference of opinion or sentiment expressed by an individual or minority. As a verb, "dissent" means to differ. "The helicopter made its *descent* into a crowd of people demonstrating their *dissent* of the government's new policy."

Desert, dessert – Though the meaning of these two nouns is distinct – "cactuses grow in the *desert*"; "we eat *dessert* after the main course" – the spelling often gets mixed up. Think of it this way: Having dessert is an extra treat that calls for a second "s." In a completely different use, "desert" as a verb (emphasis on "ert") means to leave a person or place without intending to come back. "Don't *desert* me before the wedding."

Desirous, desirable – Use "desirous" to mean having desire and "desirable" to describe a desired person or thing. "If a refreshing treat is *desirous*, you might find ice cream the most *desirable* choice."

Detract, distract – "Detract" means to take away, withdraw, hurt, or subtract. It also means to diminish the importance, value, or effectiveness of something. "Distract" means to draw the attention of the mind away; to divert. It also means to stir up or confuse with conflicting emotions or motives. It almost always acts directly on the person or thing being distracted. For example, a pile of unfinished work might "detract" you from sitting down to enjoy a football game, while a pesky mosquito might "distract" you from enjoying the game as you watch it.

Diffuse, defuse – "Diffuse" means to pour out and spread. "The spilled oil *diffused* over the kitchen counter." "Defuse" means to make less tense or dangerous. "The tense emotions became *diffused* once the expert *defused* the bomb."

Diplomat, diplomate – A "diplomat" is someone employed or skilled in diplomacy, the art and practice of conducting negotiations (e.g., between nations). A "diplomate" (dip-luh-meyt) is a person who holds a diploma, especially a physician qualified to practice a medical specialty. The final "e" implies the highest plateau of attainment in education, evaluation, excellence, and ethics. "After her graduation, now that she was a *diplomate*, she needed more than ever to be the family *diplomat* regarding her brothers' possible jealousy."

Disburse, disperse – "Disburse" means to pay out, especially from a fund; to distribute. "Disperse" means to scatter; spread widely; break up and vanish. "As soon as he had *disbursed* all the candy, the crowd of children *dispersed*."

Discomfit, discomfort – "Discomfit" means to make uneasy or perplexed; to thwart, upset, put into a state of embarrassment. This verb can lead to "discomfort" (a noun), which is an annoyance, an absence of ease; hardship, mild pain. "Even though he was innocent, Jack was *discomfited* by the prosecutor's relentless questioning, which added to his *discomfort* when confronted later by reporters outside the courtroom."

Disconsolate, inconsolable – "Disconsolate" means feeling deeply dejected and dispirited; filled with grief; inspiring dejection. "Inconsolable" (also unconsolable) takes the meaning a step further to feeling sad beyond comforting. "The *inconsolable* mother faced a *disconsolate* winter following the sudden death of her son."

Discreet, discrete – "Discreet" is being self-restrained in speech and behavior. "Discrete" refers to a separation (e.g., a company with three discrete divisions). "The rules are *discrete* (distinct) for the two groups. Be *discreet* (self-restrained) when telling others about these rules." To remember the difference, think of the "t" separating the two "e"s to create a distinction.

Disinterested, uninterested – "Disinterested" means to be impartial and unbiased. "Uninterested" means not interested, bored, indifferent. "She was *disinterested* in the outcome of the dispute and therefore made a great mediator. Her partner, however, was completely *uninterested* in the case and walked away from it."

Disparate, desperate – "Disparate" means distinct or different while "desperate" refers to having lost hope or suffering extreme need or anxiety. "With so many refugees having *disparate* dietary customs and only one type of food available, the situation became quite *desperate.*"

Disparity, discrepancy – "Disparity" and "discrepancy" both refer to a difference, but a "disparity" is an inequality of age, rank, condition, or degree, while a "discrepancy" is an inconsistency between facts or claims. "The *disparity* in age of the witnesses largely accounts for the *discrepancy* in their descriptions of the suspect: the adolescent saw an 'old man' commit the robbery, while the senior citizen described him as 'middle-aged.'"

Distinct, dissimilar – Use "distinct" when one thing can be distinguished from other things; use "dissimilar" when comparing things that are unlike or different. "The same *distinct* honor was bestowed on surprisingly *dissimilar* applicants."

Distinct, distinctive – "Distinct" means separate, dissimilar, not identical. "Silver is *distinct* from gold." "Distinctive" means having a special quality or characteristic. "The zebra's *distinctive* stripes make this animal *distinct* from others."

Distinction, discrepancy – "Distinction" often means a difference in detail that can be determined only by close inspection: e.g., the distinction between "good" and "excellent." "Discrepancy" refers to the difference between things that should correspond or match: e.g., there's a *discrepancy* between his words and his actions. "Disparity" is the condition or fact of being unequal, as in age, rank, or degree; e.g., the *disparity* (difference) between the two job offers was easy to quantify. "Although he had served his clients with *distinction*, the *discrepancy* in his personal behavior led to a *disparity* of opinion among those who knew him best."

Distress, duress – "Distress" is acute anxiety, pain, or sorrow. "Duress" refers to coercion or forced restraint. "The *duress* of being put in jail caused *distress* for the lawbreakers and their families."

Doubtful, in doubt – "Doubtful" is uncertainty about an outcome. "In doubt" is uncertainty of opinion. If the engagement is *doubtful*, that means the event is unlikely to happen. If the entertainer's engagement is *in doubt*, then no decision to hire him has been made.

Dual, duel – "Dual," an adjective, means having two of something. "Duel," a noun, refers to a fight between two people that includes the use of weapons (such as guns or swords) and usually happens while people watch. "Duel" also applies to situations in which two people or groups argue or compete with each other. As a verb, "duel" means to fight with someone using weapons, often in front of spectators. "*Dual* gunshots could be heard in the *duel* at the OK Corral."

Duplicity, duplication – "Duplicity" is intentional deception or deceit in speech or behavior; double-dealing. "Duplication" is the act, state, or product of making an exact copy of, doubling, or repeating something. "The teacher was more upset by the student's *duplicity* in volunteering to clean the chalkboards than by his subsequent *duplication* of the test answer key while in the classroom."

E

Earthy, earthly – "Earthy" consists of earth or soil; something characteristic of earth; realistic; practical; coarse or unrefined e.g., an *earthy* sense of humor. "Earthly" means worldly; something pertaining to the earth as opposed to heaven. It also means possible or conceivable e.g., an invention of no *earthly* use to anyone. "Although he appeared *earthy* and unrefined, the charlatan sweet-talked unwary widows into handing him their valuable *earthly* possessions."

Eclipse, ellipsis – "Eclipse" is the obscuring of the light of the moon by the earth coming between the moon and the sun (lunar eclipse) or the obscuring of the light of the sun by the moon coming between it and the earth (solar eclipse). As a verb, it means to surpass. "Ellipsis" is punctuation that designates a pause or missing words in a sentence. "The second-place cyclist in the Tour de France race *eclipsed* the leader in the last stage... *(ellipsis)* toward an exciting finish."

Eclectic, esoteric – As an adjective, "eclectic" describes something made up of a variety of styles, methods, ideas, cultures or historic periods; as a noun, it refers to a person who favors such an approach, especially in art or philosophy. "Esoteric" means intended for and understandable by only a small, knowledgeable group; abstruse, cryptic, enigmatic. "The gallery displayed an *eclectic* array of paintings to appeal to a wide audience, but the cryptic monotypes could only be understood by viewers with *esoteric* learning."

Edition, addition – "Edition" (noun) means one of a series of printings of the same book, newspaper, etc., each issued at a different time and differing from another. "Addition" (noun) refers to the act or process of adding (e.g., two or more numbers into one sum). "The need for many content *additions* prompted the author to publish a second *edition* of her book shortly after the first one came out."

Edition, issue – An "issue" is one of a series of something, such as a periodical or a particular month of a magazine. An "edition" is a series of printings of the same publication issued at a different time. It is often differentiated by alterations or additions not found in the original and may be limited in number (such as a "collector's edition"). It can also refer to a specific format, such as electronic, or leather-bound, or illustrated. "The book's second *edition* corrected the allegation that the June 1966 *issue* of *Collier* magazine libeled the author."

e.g., i.e., – Use "e.g.," (in Latin *exempli gratia*) when you want to say "for example" or "such as." "For the book tour, we will travel to many cities, *e.g.,* Santa Fe, Tucson, and others." "i.e.," (in Latin *id est*) means to clarify a point. It substitutes for "that is" or "namely." "The book tour includes two states, *i.e.,* New Mexico and Arizona."

Elder, older – As a noun, "elder" is someone from an earlier period, or an officer or influential member of a tribe or community. As an adjective, it refers to the older of two people or one with a higher rank. "Older," an adjective, describes something or someone having been around for many years. Note that "elder" is used when referring to people,while "older" can apply to both people and objects. "The *elder* of the two sisters had orange shag carpet in her house that was *older* than the two of them combined."

Elicit, illicit, solicit – To "elicit" (a verb) is to draw something out or bring it forth while "illicit" (an adjective) means something illegal or forbidden. To "solicit" is to try to obtain by entreaty or application; to persistently petition. "The police want to *elicit* a confession from the robber for his *illicit* behavior." "In fundraising, telling a personal story to *elicit* sympathy works better than coldly trying to *solicit* money."

Emigrate, immigrate – To remember the difference, think of "e" meaning "exit" (going out of a country) and "i" meaning "into" (coming into a country). This also applies to emigrants and immigrants. "She *emigrated* from Canada and *immigrated* into the United States. Therefore, she is a Canadian *emigrant* and a U.S. *immigrant*."

Eminent, imminent – "Eminent" refers to a distinguished person; "imminent" means something is about to happen. "The *eminent* scholar's arrival is *imminent*."

Emulate, imitate – "Emulate" means to compete with the goal of equaling or surpassing; to rival with some degree of success. "Imitate" means to follow as a model or example; to mimic, impersonate. "If you wish to *emulate* your mentor's financial success, do more than *imitate* his style of dress."

Endangered, extinct – "Endangered" means at risk of extinction; "extinct" means no longer in existence. "An *endangered* species of plants or animals becomes *extinct* when no members of the species are left on earth."

Envy, jealous – "Envy" is a longing to do or possess something that someone has done or achieved; as a verb it means to feel envy; as a noun it can also refer to the object of envy. To be "jealous" is to resent what someone has, does, or is because you want or feel you deserve it. "I *envy* my coworker's youth and beauty, and I am *jealous* that she was promoted ahead of me."

Endemic, epidemic, pandemic – "Endemic" means
prevalent in or peculiar to a locality, region, or people; a disease that occurs regularly in a particular area. "Epidemic" means spreading extensively by infection, affecting many individuals in an area or population at the same time; a rapid spread in any occurrence. "Pandemic" refers to an epidemic in a wide geographical area affecting a large proportion of the population. "Malaria is *endemic* to the tropics." An *epidemic* of cholera tends to occur after a natural disaster causes sanitation to break down." "At the time the H1N1 virus was declared a *pandemic*, infections had been reported in more than 70 countries."

Enervate, energize – "Enervate" means to deprive of
strength or vitality; weaken physically or mentally; debilitate. In medicine, it means to remove a nerve or nerve part. To "energize" is to give energy to; rouse into activity; to supply electrical current to something. "The speeches were aimed at *energizing* the crowd, but their depressing message had the effect of *enervating* any desire to take action

Enormousness, enormity – "Enormousness" describes
something great in size or extent. "Enormity" means a monstrous offense or evil. "The *enormousness* of the cleanup required after the storm wasn't yet known." "Not until journalists were able to enter Cambodia did the world become aware of the *enormity* of Pol Pot's oppression." *Note:* Some sources advise limiting the use of "enormity" to situations demanding a negative moral judgment although not all sources agree.

Ensure, assure, insure

Ensure – To make sure something happens. "I will research your audience thoroughly to *ensure* a customized presentation."

Assure – To make someone feel sure about something. "I want to *assure* you I will customize the presentation so it fits your audience."

Insure – To buy an insurance policy for financial protection in case something happens. "I *insure* my business against liability and theft."

Entropy, atrophy – "Entropy" is a measure of the disorder or randomness of a system; the steady deterioration of a society or system. As a noun, "atrophy" is the wasting away of a body organ or tissue; deterioration from disuse. As a verb, "atrophy" means to waste away or deteriorate. "I dislike housework and exercising, but without them, neatness will give way to *entropy* and my muscles will start to *atrophy*."

Evasive, invasive – "Evasive" means intentionally avoiding something or being vague or ambiguous, while "invasive" refers to intruding or encroaching (upon privacy or in armed aggression), or spreading into healthy tissue (e.g., invasive surgery). "The doctor's curt answers were *evasive* because he was reluctant to tell his patient about her *invasive* carcinoma."

Every day, everyday – In the two-word adverbial phrase, "day" refers to the time between sunrise and sunset; "every" describes the word day. "*Every day* we call our customers." Everyday (without a space) is an adjective that precedes the noun it describes. "It's an *everyday* occurrence."

Evoke, provoke – "Evoke" means to call up or produce memories, feelings, etc. or to elicit or draw forth. "Provoke" is more assertive. It means to anger, enrage, stir up, arouse, or to induce feelings, desires, or actions. "His shocking comment *evoked* protests from students who *provoked* a riot in the street."

Evoke, invoke – "Evoke" means to summon, call up, produce memories, feelings or to elicit or draw forth. "Invoke" has a religious connotation, to call in (e.g., a deity), also to declare binding (e.g., invoke a law). "*Invoking* God's help during tough times can *evoke* feelings of peace."

Exacerbate, exasperate – To "exacerbate" is to increase the severity, bitterness, or violence of something. To "exasperate" is to irritate, annoy, or provoke someone to a high degree. "By trying to fix the sink himself, he only *exacerbated* the problem and *exasperated* his wife into calling the plumber herself."

Exaggerate, exacerbate – To "exaggerate" is to make overstatements or to increase to an abnormal degree. To "exacerbate" is to aggravate an already difficult or severe situation. "If you *exaggerate*, people may stop believing you." "Drought and high winds *exacerbate* the wildfire in the mountains."

Except, accept – "Except" means leaving something or someone out while "accept" means agreeing to something. "*Except* for Tom, I can *accept* all the other candidates on the slate."

Exodus, migration – An "exodus" is a mass departure. "Migration" is the act or process of migrating. To migrate means to move from one location to another or to pass periodically from one region or climate. In effect, an exodus is a forced migration. "The tribe planned a *migration* south for the winter, but rival tribes invaded their village and forced an *exodus* before they could get their belongings together."

Expedient, expeditious – "Expedient" as an adjective refers to something that's done for short-term gain suiting one's own self-interest. "Expedient/expediency" as a noun means action used to meet an urgent need. "Expeditious" is acting with speed and efficiency. "In today's political climate, radio stations find it *expedient* to play patriotic songs." "Urgent situations require *expeditious* handling of supplies."

Extend, expand – "Extend" means to stretch or lengthen, or to draw out up to full length; also to present or offer, as in a greeting or contribution. "Expand" means to spread out, develop, or otherwise enlarge in size or scope, etc. "If your waist *expands*, you have to *extend* your belt length."

Extort, exhort – To "extort" is to use intimidation to obtain something; to "exhort" is to use strong argument or appeal to prompt someone to take action. "I *exhort* you to tell me the truth so I won't have to *extort* it from you through blackmail."

Exult, exalt – "Exult" means to rejoice greatly, be jubilant or triumphant. "Exalt" means to raise in rank, character, or status; to elevate. "The locals *exulted* when their candidate won the national election, hoping the added exposure would finally *exalt* their town's reputation in the nation's eyes."

Fail, flail – "Fail" is to fall short of achievement in something expected, attempted, desired, or approved. "The experiment will *fail* if you don't plan." It also means to receive less than the passing mark in an exam, class, or course of study. The verb "flail" means to beat or strike as if with a "flail" (a tool for threshing grain). "We *flailed* our horses with the reins." It also means to thrash about, moving vigorously or erratically. "The boxers *flailed* at each other in the ring."

Famous, notorious – "Famous" means known widely and favorably, while "notorious" means known widely and unfavorably. "The young actress became *famous* for her Oscar-nominated role, and then became *notorious* for her drug use and underage drinking."

Farther, further – "Farther" refers to a geographic distance. "Further" reflects reasoning and is used with intangibles like time, quantity, etc. "Thinking about this *further*, I know I can drive *farther* today than yesterday." Use "farther" when referring to a physical distance. Use "further" to refer to abstract ideas or indicate a greater extent or degree.

Fatal, fateful – "Fatal" means capable of causing death, disaster, or destruction. "Fateful" refers to being controlled by fate, predetermined, portentous. "The vivid nightmare proved to be *fateful* for the driver who died in a *fatal* car crash a day later."

Faze, phase, phase in – "Faze" (verb) means to cause one to be disturbed or disconcerted. "Phase" (used as a verb) refers to scheduling or ordering something so it's available when needed. "Phase in" means to put into use, gradually. "So that starting a writing project doesn't *faze* her, she's learned to explore her ideas on paper first and *phase in* the review stage later."

Fewer, less – "Fewer" is used when units or individuals can be counted; less is used with quantities of mass, bulk, or volume. "There are *fewer* letters to be written today than yesterday." "The mail takes up *less* space than I thought it would." Generally, if the word has an "s" at the end, use "fewer" – fewer dollars but less money; fewer muffins but less food.

Fictitious, fictional – "Fictitious" means created, taken, or assumed for the sake of concealment; not genuine; false. "Fictional" as an adjective refers to the class of literature comprising works of imaginative narration in prose form. "Wanting to hide his identity, he used a *fictitious* name borrowed from a *fictional* character in his favorite novel."

Figurative, literal – "Figurative" refers to the metaphoric nature of an object while its opposite "literal" refers to its strict definition. Use "figurative" as a fancy figure of speech and "literal" as a straight interpretation. "Be *literal* in your feedback about his use of *figurative* language."

Financial, fiscal – "Financial" is used when talking about monetary receipts, expenditures, credit, transactions, or operations. "Fiscal" pertains to the public treasury, government revenues or debt, or to the monetary policies of an organization. "The Board of Trustees re-evaluated the organization's *fiscal* policies after witnessing continued poor performance on the *financial* statements."

Flaunt, flout – "Flaunt" means to show off. "Flout" means to defy or ignore. "When he *flaunted* his fast, new sports car, he *flouted* the highway speed limit."

Foment, ferment – "Foment" is a verb that means to instigate or foster (e.g., discord, rebellion); to promote the growth or development of; to apply warm water, medicated liquid, or ointments to the skin. As a verb, "ferment" means to cause or undergo fermentation (e.g., conversion of grape sugar to alcohol by yeast); to be in or cause an agitated or excited state; as a noun, it means agitation or unrest; something that causes fermentation. "The charismatic speaker was so successful at *fomenting* rebellion that the ensuing political *ferment* quickly led to the collapse of the regime."

Forbid, prohibit – Use "forbid" with "to" and "prohibit" with "from." It's correct to say, "She was *prohibited* from attending" but it's incorrect to say, "She was prohibited to attend." Instead, say, "She was *forbidden* to attend."

Formally, formerly – "Formally" means to follow accepted forms, conventions, or regulations. "Formerly" means having occurred at an earlier time. "She *formally* invited us to the party with embossed linen invitations. While unusual in modern times, such invitations were *formerly* the norm."

Forward, foreword – "Forward" can be an adverb, adjective, noun or verb, all related to movement toward a front. "Foreword" (a noun) is the section found at the front of a book. To remember the correct spelling, separate "foreword" into "fore" (to go before) and "word" (the words/ideas that follow).

Fortunate, fortuitous – "Fortunate" means lucky while "fortuitous" means happening by chance. "I needed to talk with Mary, so seeing her in the store was *fortuitous*. Because she gave me good news, our meeting was also *fortunate*."

Foundering, floundering – "Floundering" describes something struggling clumsily, confusedly, or helplessly. "Foundering" describes a boat filling with water and sinking, ground or a building sinking down, or a horse stumbling and going lame. "We tried to save both the man *floundering* in the river and his horse *foundering* in deep mud along the bank."

Frightful, frightened – "Frightful" refers to causing disgust, fright, shock; horrifying. "Frightened" means to be alarmed, filled with fear. "News of a *frightful* tornado about to sweep into the town *frightened* the residents into evacuating."

Gate, gait – A "gate" is a movable barrier, often on hinges, a means of access or egress. "Gait" is a manner of walking, stepping or running, especially the way a horse moves. To "gait" is to teach a horse a specific way of walking. "Rather than dismount to open the *gate*, the rider changed the horse's *gait* from a trot to a gallop."

Gambol, gamble – "Gambol" as a verb is to frolic, skip about playfully. As a noun, it means skipping or leaping about happily. "Gamble" means to play at any game of chance for money or other stakes, to stake or risk anything of value on the outcome of something involving chance. "In opening a new store, the owners *gamble* it will be a success, and when it is, they'll *gambol* with delight."

Gauge, gouge – As a noun, a "gauge" is a unit or instrument of measure. As a verb, it means to measure precisely, evaluate or judge. "I use the bathroom scale so I can gauge the number of pounds I've dropped." A "gouge" is a chisel used to scoop out a hole. It's also the action of using a gouge. Metaphorically, it means to scoop out too much. "He used a *gauge* designed for woodworking to *gouge* holes in the ground for irrigation."

Genial, congenial – "Genial" describes a gracious manner contributing to a pleasant experience while "congenial" refers to an agreeable disposition, someone's nature. "The host created a *genial* atmosphere for the *congenial* friends who gathered at the party."

Glimpse, glance – "Glance" (a verb) refers to taking a fast look at something while a "glimpse" (a noun) is the act of seeing something quickly. "I *glance* over my shoulder to catch a *glimpse* of traffic behind me."

Gorilla, guerilla – A "gorilla" is a species of large ape, or a brutish person or thug. A "guerilla" is a member of a group of irregular soldiers who usually operate in small groups to harass their enemy with surprise raids or sabotage. As an adjective, it describes their style of warfare. "Peacefully foraging *gorillas* may get caught in the crossfire when *guerillas* wage war in the animals' habitat."

Gourmand, gourmet – Both of these people love food, but a "gourmand" tends to be a greedy or ravenous eater while a "gourmet" is devoted to refined, sensuous enjoyment. "Charles, who sees himself as a *gourmet*, savored every bite of his meal while his *gourmand* companion devoured everything on his plate and asked for more."

Gratuity, gratuitous – A "gratuity" is a favor or gift, usually money, given for service; a tip. "Gratuitous" means unnecessary, unwarranted, or unjustified; less commonly it means given or obtained without charge or payment. "The waiter's excellent service was rewarded with a generous *gratuity*." "I prefer movies that aren't filled with *gratuitous* sex and violence."

Grudge, grunge – A "grudge" refers to a resentment or a harboring of ill feelings. "Grunge" is the state of being covered with dirt or unclean things. It's also a type of rock music or style of dress that blends elements of punk rock and heavy metal. "Cindy's mother held a *grudge* toward her for years because Cindy wore *grunge* clothing as a teenager."

H

Hanged, hung – Use "hanged" when referring to people; use "hung" for everything else. "The prisoner was *hanged* for his crime." "The wet clothes were *hung* outside to dry."

Harangue, harass – "Harangue" (noun or verb) refers to a tirade or rant, such as a long, pompous speech delivered to an assembly or directed at an individual. "Harass" means to disturb, torment, bother continually, pester; persecute. "Unable to *harangue* the citizenry by giving speeches openly, the rebellious leader chose to *harass* people on the street."

Hardy, hearty – "Hardy" describes being bold, sturdy, courageous, or capable of enduring hardship. "Hearty" means warm-hearted, genuine, sincere. "The *hardy* athletes received *hearty* congratulations after winning the grueling game." "Hearty" can also mean forceful (a hearty push), substantial (a hearty meal), vigorous (a hearty workout).

Healthful, wholesome – "Healthful" implies a positive contribution to a healthy condition (get involved in healthful exercise) while "wholesome" applies to something that benefits you, builds you up, or sustains you. "Louisa May Alcott wrote: 'Work is *wholesome* . . . it keeps us from ennui and mischief. Work, however, is not always *healthful!*'"

Hone, home in – To "hone" is to sharpen, to make clear or precise. To "home in" is to aim or direct onto a point or target. You can hone a point but you home in on a target.

"It's important to *hone* your message so readers can *home in* on exactly what you mean."

Hope, wish – "Hope" is a noun or verb concerning a feeling that what you desire is possible or that events will turn out for the best. "Wish" is a noun or verb pertaining to wanting, desiring, or longing for something. "We *hope* you have a wonderful career; we *wish* you good luck." "I ignored my mother's *wish*, and now I have no *hope* of becoming a doctor."

Hurdle, hurtle, hurl – "Hurdle" as a noun is a barrier, wall, fence over which a runner or animal leaps; a difficult problem to be overcome. As a verb, it means to leap over, master. "Hurtle" means to rush violently, move with great speed, go noisily with violent or rapid motion. "Hurl" is to throw something forcefully. "After *hurdling* the net to offer his opponent a consoling embrace, the new singles tennis champ *hurled* his wrist bands into the crowd and *hurtled* through the throng of courtside photographers to hug his coach."

I

Illustrious, illustrative – "Illustrious" refers to someone who is highly distinguished, renowned, or famous. "Illustrative" refers to clarifying a point by example or demonstration. "*Illustrious* presenters rise above the others because they use *illustrative* stories to bring their ideas alive."

Immolate, emulate – "Immolate" means to kill as a sacrificial victim; to kill (oneself) by fire. "Emulate" means to strive to equal or excel, especially through imitation; to rival with some degree of success. "The Buddhist monks who *immolated* themselves in 1963 to protest the persecution of Buddhists in South Vietnam were later *emulated* by protestors of the Vietnam War."

Impassible, impassable – "Impassible" means showing no emotion. "Impassable" means not being able to pass (e.g., on a road) or not being able to overcome (e.g., an obstacle). "As we waited for the *impassable* road to be cleared of snow, George remained *impassible*, refusing to get upset about the long delay."

Impetuous, impulsive – Both words refer to people who are hasty or precipitate in their actions. The difference comes from the intention, or lack thereof, behind the action. "Impetuous" suggests eagerness, impatience, recklessness, or rashness, while "impulsive" emphasizes spontaneity and a lack of reflection or forethought. Think of the word impatient when you think of "impetuous." By comparison, "impulsive" actions tend to be motivated by emotion rather than thought; they are often sudden and sometimes ill advised. "His *impetuous* advances made her feel *impulsive* about getting away from him."

Implode, explode – "Implode" means to collapse inward in a violent way. "Explode" is to release energy or burst or break up violently and noisily. "When demolishing a building, engineers use dynamite in a particular way to make it *implode* while not letting it *explode*."

Imply, infer – The one who initiates a communication "implies" while a receiver or observer "infers." "The reader *inferred* the politician's actions were immoral. The editorial writer intended to *imply* that."

Incisive, insightful – "Incisive" means penetrating, clear, or sharp; sometimes that sharpness verges on being biting or sarcastic. "Insightful" means being perceptive, understanding the true inner nature of a situation, thing, or person. "His *incisive* review of the documentary was more than *insightful*; its sarcasm revealed the reviewer's political bias."

Incongruity, incongruency *(not a real word)* – "Incongruity" refers to the quality of disagreeing, being unsuitable or inappropriate. "Incongruency" is not correct.

Incredulous, incredible – "Incredulous" means skeptical, disbelieving." "Incredible" means so implausible as to elicit disbelief; often used simply to express amazement. "They were *incredulous* after hearing about the *incredible* tidal wave of destruction."

Inequality, inequity – "Inequality" is the state or quality of being unequal; an instance of disparity, difference. "Inequity" refers to unfairness; favoritism or bias; an unfair circumstance. "A modern-day *inequity* includes the rising *inequality* of income between rich and poor."

Inevitable, invariable – "Inevitable" means can't be avoided or escaped from. "Invariable" refers to being constant and unchangeable. "Her style of playing tennis was steady and *invariable*, but her *inevitable* mistakes cost her the victory."

Infallible, fallible – "Infallible" means incapable of erring or failing, while "fallible" means just the opposite—capable of making an error. "It's impossible to create an *infallible* system because systems are designed by humans who are *fallible*."

Infringe, impinge – "Infringe" means to transgress, exceed a limit, or violate. "Impinge" means to collide, strike, encroach, or trespass. "I was legally wronged when they *infringed* on my patent rights. I felt endangered when they *impinged* on my privacy."

Ingenious, ingenuous – "Ingenious" means character- ized by cleverness or originality in contriving something new as in an ingenious device. "Ingenuous" means candid or innocent; free from reserve, restraint; sincere; e.g., a thug with the ingenuous eyes of a choirboy. "It was *ingenious* how the criminal feigned *ingenuous* characteristics to avoid making the detective suspicious."

Injured, wounded – In the adjective form, "injured" refers to something or someone who has been wronged, harmed, or impaired; "wounded" refers to something or someone who has been injured by a weapon, feels emotional pain, or suffers from an action intended to be hurtful. In the verb form, "to wound" and "to injure" are similar. The difference becomes clearer in the noun form. A "wound" is a specific type of injury—medically speaking, one in which the skin is broken or tissue damaged. A "wound" typically results from harmful intent whereas an "injury" occurs by accident or circumstance. "The passengers on the bus were *injured* in the crash that happened after the driver was *wounded* by a crazed man wielding a knife."

Insidious, invidious – "Insidious" refers to something harmfully enticing or stealthily treacherous and having a gradual and subtle effect. "Invidious" refers to feelings of animosity, discontent, resentment, or to obnoxious, even harmful behavior; something likely to cause bad feelings. "Hurricanes are especially *insidious* when they strike unpredictably." "The doorman's *invidious* remark angered him even more after he got kicked out of the nightclub."

Insight, incite – "Insight" is the result of seeing into the inner meaning of a situation or a person's motives or behavior. "Incite" is a verb meaning to stir up action. "Seeing the rebel leaders *incite* a riot gave the reporter *insight* into the frustration they felt."

Insular, isolated – "Insular" refers to a characteristic of people who are secluded, especially those having a narrow, provincial viewpoint. "Isolated" refers to something that occurs once; unique; sporadic. It can also mean set apart or quarantined from others, which is similar to "insular." "Isolated" refers to the action while "insular" refers to the result of that action. "Diagnosed with polio at a young age, she had few friends and lived quite *isolated*. This resulted in her developing an *insular* view of the world."

Intense, intensive – Both adjectives refer to an extreme in degree, strength, or intensity. "Intense" arises from within while "intensive" is imposed from without. "Because of her *intense* feelings for her daughter, the mother lavishes *intensive* attention on her."

Interment, internment – "Interment" is the act or ceremony of burial. "Internment" is confinement, especially of enemy citizens in wartime. "Having witnessed the *interment* of those shot because they attempted to escape, he resolved to tolerate life in the *internment* camp."

Interpolate, extrapolate – To "interpolate" is to introduce something new between existing parts, especially in the sense of inserting foreign material to falsify a text. To "extrapolate" is to infer or estimate by extending or projecting known information. "The corrupt accountant *interpolated* fabricated records into the yearly earnings report so positive growth would be *extrapolated* for the next quarter."

Intimate, intimidate – "Intimate" (an adjective pronounced with a short 'a') means interconnected or highly personal; private. "We have an *intimate* friendship." "Intimate" (a verb pronounced with long 'a') means to hint at or suggest. "He *intimated* resigning his job." "Intimidate" means to threaten. "The bully *intimidated* everyone in the class."

Intimation, imitation – An "intimation" is a subtle hint or suggestion. An "imitation" is a counterfeit or inferior copy of a genuine item. "She thought her friend's *intimation* would be about boys, but instead she admitted her handbag was an *imitation*."

Into, in to – "Into" refers to entering something (go *into* the legal profession); changing a form (turn lemons *into* lemonade); making contact (run *into* a doorjamb). "In to" are two prepositions that come together, as in: "Let's go *in to* have breakfast." Hint: If your sentence still makes sense when you drop the "in," use two separate words. "Let's go (in) to have breakfast."

Intrusive, obtrusive – They both describe something or someone as disruptive, adverse, or prominent in an unwelcome way. The difference lies in the implied direction of each word. "Intrusive" implies thrusting into a place or situation, while "obtrusive" implies thrusting out beyond accepted or expected limits. "At the opening, the artist was attentive to his guests without being *obtrusive*. I can't say the same for the *intrusive* gallery owner who repeatedly interrupted the patrons' conversations."

Innovation, invention – "Innovation" refers to something that has not been thought of or created before. "Invention" is something developed through process and experimentation. "The *invention* of the washing machine was touted as a great *innovation* of its time."

Irregardless, regardless – Most references do not consider "irregardless" a word even though it's often heard in speech. Some include it, but state that "irregardless" is not generally accepted. Always use "regardless," which means in spite of. "He will go on the trip *regardless* of the dangers."

Irritate, aggravate – "Irritate" means to annoy. "Aggravate" means to make worse. "I *aggravated* the situation when I *irritated* the leaders by asking irrelevant questions."

It's, its – Use an apostrophe when you can logically substitute "it's" for "it is" in a sentence. Otherwise, use "its." "*It's* easy to remember to put the book in *its* place."

Jocular, jugular – "Jocular" means characterized by joking. "Jugular" refers to the region around the neck or throat. Metaphorically, it means going for a kill or strike. "Though his comments were meant to sound *jocular*, he aimed his criticism at the *jugular*."

Junction, juncture – A "junction" is a place where two things (especially roads or tracks) meet, come together, or join. A "juncture" is a critical point in time; the line or point where two objects or forces intersect. "The old station building near the railway *junction* has become a safety hazard. At this a critical *juncture*, we must either preserve it as a historic site or tear it down."

L

Lay, lie – The verb "lay" always has an object, just like the verb "put" always has an object. "Please *lay* (put) the plate on the table." The verb "lie" doesn't take an object. "*Lie* down if you feel tired." Confusion happens because the past tense of "lie" is "lay." "Today, I *lie* down; yesterday I lay down." The past tense of "lay" (put) is "laid" and it still requires an object (the plate). "Yesterday, I *laid* (put) the plate beside his bed after he *lay* down."

Lead, led – The verb "lead" (with a long "e") means to show the way. "The guides *lead* a hiking group every Saturday." The past tense of this verb "led" (with a short "e") is spelled with three letters, not four. "They *led* the hike yesterday." Confusion occurs because the noun "lead" (a pencil lead) is pronounced the same as "led."

Learn, teach – "Learn" indicates knowledge or behavior is being acquired. "Teach" indicates knowledge is being provided by someone. "Students are wise to *learn* the lessons their instructors *teach*."

Leech, leach – A "leech" is a blood-sucking worm used in medicine for bloodletting or a person who clings to another person and uses up his or her resources. As a verb, it describes such behavior. To "leach" (verb) is to dissolve out the soluble components of something by percolating liquid; to empty or drain. The noun refers to the process of material being leached. "Although she'd considered her stepmother a gold-digging *leech* and was glad she divorced her father, it seemed to *leach* all the joy out of his life."

Less, small, fewer – When size is involved, use "small"; when importance is involved, use "less"; when quantity is involved, use "few" or "fewer." Also, if you can count the number of items, use "fewer." "The *small* dog picked the *less* painful of two options. He faced *fewer* obstacles by retreating than by attacking the porcupine."

Lightning, lightening – The electrical bolts in the sky refer to "lightning" (without an 'e'). When the dark skies are "lightening" after a storm, the word has an 'e' because it comes from the verb "lighten," meaning to be less heavy, less dark, less burdensome. "After the *lightning* storm passes, we see the sky *lightening* up."

Loath, loathe – "Loath" is an adjective that means unwilling. "Loathe" is a verb that means to abhor or hate. "I felt *loath* to admit the accident was my fault because I *loathe* feeling out of control."

Lose, loose – The verb "lose" is the opposite of the verb "win." "Do you win or *lose* when you gamble?" The adjective "loose" means not fastened tightly while the verb "loose" means to free something. "This *loose* blouse looks comfortable." "*Loose* (or loosen) your tie and relax!" Confusion occurs because the pronunciation differs from what's expected: "lose" with one "o" has a longer "ooh" sound than "loose" with two "o's."

Lurking, lurching – "Lurking" means to lie in wait; be sneaky. "Lurching" is a staggering or tottering movement. "At first, she thought the noise came from her dog *lurking* around the corner. She quickly realized it came from her cat, *lurching* to free itself from being tangled in a trash bag."

Lurk, lure – "Lurk" means lying in wait for someone, hiding for a sinister purpose; existing unobserved or unsuspected. "Lure" means attracting, enticing, or tempting someone into a wrong or foolish course, especially by using something desirable as bait. "Hansel and Gretel couldn't see the witch *lurk* inside the gingerbread house, attempting to *lure* children in to eat them."

Luxurious, luxuriant – "Luxurious" means pertaining to luxury. "They live in a *luxurious* home." "Luxuriant" means profuse growth or display. "Tropical vegetation is *luxuriant*." "She has *luxuriant* brown hair." These two words are given as synonyms in the dictionary, but in common usage, the distinction is apparent.

Manner, manor – " Manner" is the way in which a thing is done or happens. "Manor" means the district over which a lord had domain in medieval times. "I learned the right *manner* of using a battering ram at Lord Byron's *manor* this fortnight."

Martial, marital, marshal – "Martial" relates to being aggressive and warlike; it's associated with armed forces. "Marital" refers to marriage. "Marshal" as a noun refers to certain military, judicial, and police or fire officers. As a verb, it means to arrange in order, assemble and organize or lead ceremoniously. "Although he acted like a *martial* warrior at work, his *marital* demeanor at home was loving and docile." "After Pearl Harbor was bombed and Hawaii was put under *martial* law, the commander had authority to *marshal* all available resources."

Meat, mete – "Meat" is the edible part of anything (animal, fruit, nut). It also refers to the essential point made in speaking or writing. As a verb, "mete" means to distribute or apportion by measure; allot; dole out. As a noun, it means a limiting mark. "The person who *metes* out the *meat* at the holiday meal often delivers the *meat* of the day's message."

Meddlesome, nettlesome – "Meddlesome" means being inclined to interfere. "Nettlesome" means causing annoyance. "Her mother-in-law's *meddlesome* nature was a *nettlesome* thorn in the couple's marriage."

Militate, mitigate – "Militate" means to have a substantial effect or influence on. "Mitigate" means to lessen or make less severe; to moderate a quality or condition. "He knew his weak grades would *militate* against him, but he hoped to *mitigate* their effect with a brilliant college application essay and strong SAT scores."

Mischievous, mischievious *(not a real word)* – "Mischievous" means causing mischief or being playful in a teasing way. "Mischievious" is an incorrect pronunciation and spelling of mischievous. "The *mischievous* father enjoyed instigating spats among family members at Sunday dinner."

Miscreant, recreant – "Miscreant" as an adjective means depraved, villainous, and base; as a noun, it refers to a vicious or depraved person. "Recreant" as an adjective means cowardly, unfaithful, disloyal, and traitorous. It can also be a noun meaning a coward or renegade. "Today's horror movies feature *miscreants* who like to torture people." "The *recreant* deserter fled before the battle and joined the other side after it won."

Momento, memento – While "momento" is not a word, it's commonly misused in place of "memento"—a reminder of the past, a keepsake. To avoid tripping up, remember the word "memory"; the first vowel is "e" (not "o" as in "moment"). "Buy a *memento* of San Francisco so you'll remember your trip."

Moot, mute – "Moot" (rhymes with "boot") as an adjective means open to discussion; debatable; doubtful, academic, not practical. It also means of no particular significance. Thus, depending on context, a *moot* point can be debated but has no actual significance or one that is pointless. As a verb, it means to make a point theoretical, to bring up a subject for discussion. "Mute" (rhymes with "cute") means silent or incapable of speech; a person who does not speak. As a verb, it means to make silent. "Knowing how to *mute* the stereo speakers becomes a *moot* point once you discover they haven't been plugged in."

Moral, morale – "Moral" is concerned with the principles or rules of right conduct, ethics, distinction between right and wrong. "Morale" is the emotional or mental state of a group indicating high spirits, confidence, zeal, especially in the face of opposition or hardship. "The *morale* of the troops went down when they witnessed low *moral* behavior from their leaders." "The *moral* of the story encourages team members to keep their *morale* high."

Moribund, morbid – "Moribund" describes approaching death, or on the verge of becoming obsolete. "Morbid" means relating to or caused by disease, or characterized by gloominess. "Buying stock in *moribund* businesses is likely to have a *morbid* effect on one's portfolio."

National, nationwide – "National" means pertaining to or belonging to a nation, or relating to one's nationality. "Nationwide" describes something existing throughout a whole nation (synonymous with "across the country"). "The downturn of the *national* economy concerned wage earners *nationwide*."

Navel, naval – "Navel" refers to the umbilicus (belly button) or the central or middle portion of something. "Naval" means pertaining to ships, warships, or a navy. "The toddler was too fascinated by his own *navel* to notice the epic *naval* battle his brother was staging with toy ships."

Number, amount – You've likely heard people say, "Consider the amount of stores or the amount of muffins, etc." In these phrases, the word "number" should be used instead of "amount." Hint: If you can quantify or count the objects, use "number," not "amount." Therefore, the correct phrases are "Consider the *number* of stores, the *number* of muffins, etc."

Obstinate, stubborn – "Obstinate" connotes rigid thinking or persistent behavior and is often used negatively. "Stubborn" indicates a resistance to change that may or may not be admirable. "Contrary to the evidence, he was *obstinate* in his belief that the suspect was guilty. This time, his *stubbornness* didn't pay off."

Officious, official – "Officious" means being excessively eager in offering services or advice where not requested or needed; meddlesome. As a noun, an "official' is a person appointed or elected to an office. As an adjective, it pertains to an office or position of authority. "In the guise of making an *official* call to the shop, the thief posed as a cop and kept asking *officious* questions.

Oneiric, onerous – "Oneiric" relates to dreams while "onerous" means troublesome, oppressive, burdensome. "The *oneiric* writing revealed the poet's *onerous* inner life."

Over, more than – "Over" implies a geographic position. "More than" means an increased number. "The lamp hangs *over* the table." "*More than* 400 people stayed for the second show." (As our language changes, though, "over" has become commonly accepted for both uses.)

P

Palate, palette, pallet – "Palate" refers to the roof of the mouth and one's sense of taste. "Palette" is a board used by painters for holding and mixing colors. It also refers to the range of colors used by artists. "Viewing a painting created from the *palette* of a fine artist enhances the appeal of gourmet food on one's *palate*." "Pallet" is a small, low platform on which goods are stored or moved. "Cartons of canned goods are delivered to the store on a *pallet*."

Paramount, tantamount – "Paramount" means chief in importance or impact; supreme; preeminent; superior in power or jurisdiction. "Tantamount" refers to an equivalent as in value, force, effect, or significance. "By getting half-drunk before a televised debate, the senator committed an act of *paramount* folly, *tantamount* to dropping the Mother of all Bombs on his political future."

Parody, parity – "Parody" is a humorous or satirical imitation of a serious piece of communication. As a verb, it means to imitate another for the purpose of ridicule or satire. "Parity" refers to equality, as in amount, status, or character. "In an effort to create *parity*, the organization revised its rules but succeeded only in making a *parody* of the original rules."

Passed, past – "Passed" is a form of the verb "pass" meaning to go by. "I *pass* the mailbox on my way to work every day. Yesterday, I *passed* it more times than usual." "Past" is an adjective, noun, preposition, or adverb that shows something has gone by. Adj.: "We celebrate *past* glories." Noun: "We enjoy thinking about the *past*." Preposition: "It's the house just *past* the corner." Adverb: "The troops marched *past*."

Peak, pique, peek – "Peak" refers to the top of something (e.g., a mountain, chart). "Pique" means to attract someone's interest. "Peek" means to take a quick look at something. "I want to *pique* your interest in climbing to the *peak* of that mountain so we can *peek* at the valley on the other side."

Pedal, peddle – The verb "pedal" refers to riding a bicycle while "peddle" means to sell something. "The salesman *peddles* new products every week as he *pedals* his bike through the neighborhood."

Personnel, personal – "Personnel" is a noun referring to people employed at an organization. "Personal," an adjective, means private matters relating to a particular person. "The candidate said the *personnel* at the newspaper focused more on her *personal* characteristics than on his political stance."

Perspective, prospective – "Perspective" as a noun refers to spatial relationships, a mental view of facts, ideas, etc. "Prospective" as an adjective addresses future or expected outcomes. "From his boss's *perspective*, Sam's *prospective* promotion looks doubtful."

Persuasive, pervasive – "Persuasive" means having the ability to influence or convince. "Pervasive" means widespread or diffused throughout. "A used car salesman's ability to be *persuasive* doesn't work with customers who have experienced deceptions that are *pervasive* in the industry."

Pitcher, picture – A "pitcher" throws the ball during a baseball game; it's also a container that holds liquid. A "picture" is a visual image. "The team's ace *pitcher* is the *picture* of good sportsmanship. Let's celebrate with a *pitcher* of lemonade."

Plod, plot – "Plod" means to move or walk heavily or laboriously. As a noun, "plot" is a small piece of ground, or story told in a novel, play, or movie, or a chart or map showing the movements or progress of an object; as a verb, "plot" means to a plan for or scheme, or make a diagram of. "We watched her *plod* through her snow-covered *plot* and wondered about her *plot* for making plants grow in the middle of winter."

Populous, populace – "Populous" is an adjective meaning full of inhabitants; densely populated. "Populace" is a noun referring to those inhabitants, the general public, especially the common people as opposed to higher classes. "As the city grew more *populous* and no additional housing was built, the *populace* grew discontent."

Pour, pore – "Pour" means to send a substance falling into a container (they *pour* some drinks) and to proceed in great numbers (spectators *pour* out of the stadium). "Pore" as a verb refers to reading with steady attention and is usually followed by the word "over." "She *pored* over old manuscripts to find the answer."

Practical, practicable – "Practical" consists of, involves, or results from practice or action (e.g., a practical application of a rule). "Practicable" means feasible, capable of being put into practice with available means (e.g., a practicable solution).

> **Slight but significant distinctions:** Something practical is *useful* while something practicable is *usable*. Practical refers to anything that can be done and *is worth doing;*

practicable pertains to anything that can be done, worthwhile or not. "The general wanted a *practical* method to ford the river so his engineers found material nearby to build a *practicable* solution."

Precede, proceed – To "precede" is to go before while "proceed" is to go forward. "When good planning *precedes* any trip, you can *proceed* to have a wonderful time."

Premier, premiere – "Premier" as an adjective means first in status or importance, first to occur or exist. As a noun, it refers to a chief administrative officer, as of a province. "Premiere" as a noun is the first public performance, as of a movie or play. As a verb, it means to present that first public performance. "The *premier* cast members *premiere* in a special performance of the striking new play, which will be attended by the *premier* of the province."

Prescribe, proscribe – "Prescribe" is to establish a rule or guideline; in a medical sense, to order medicine or treatment. "Proscribe" is to banish, condemn, or prohibit. "The judge decided to *prescribe* an alcohol treatment program for the offender rather than *proscribe* his ability to drive by taking his license away."

Presume, assume – Both imply taking something for granted but "assume" means supposing something is true while "presume" shows a stronger belief implying unwarranted boldness. "I *assume* he'll arrive when he says he will." "Well, don't *presume* you're always right."

Presumptive, presumptuous – "Presumptive" means to provide a reasonable basis for belief or acceptance. "Presumptuous" means going beyond what is proper; impertinent, audacious, arrogant. "The *presumptuous* teenager asked to stay out all night, but his argument wasn't *presumptive* enough for his parents to say yes."

Preventive, preventative – Both of these words mean serving to prevent or hinder but, for simplicity, "preventive" is preferred over "preventative." "We work with doctors who use a *preventive* approach to treating their patients."

Principal, principle – "Principal" as a noun means head of a school, a main participant, or a sum of money. As an adjective, it means highest in value or rank. "Principle" is a fundamental law or basic truth. "The school *principal* lives by her values and *principles*." "The *principal* issue is calculating the *principal* plus interest correctly."

Probable, possible – "Probable" refers to what is *likely* to happen or be true. "Possible" refers to what *can* happen or be true. If you say something is probable, you're expressing more confidence it will happen than if you state it's possible. "It's *possible* for anyone to become extremely wealthy, but is it *probable* more than one percent of the population will achieve a high level of financial wealth?"

Probability, possibility – "Probability" is the chance that something may occur, often expressed statistically. "Possibility" refers to the fact that something can happen. "The *probability* that humans will inhabit the moon in significant numbers is low, but it's still a theoretical *possibility*."

Prognosis, prognostication – While "prognosis" and "prognostication" both mean a forecast or prediction, "prognosis" specifically refers to the probable course or outcome of a disease, especially the likelihood of recovery. "The *prognosis* for many cancers is good if they are detected early." "Before daily weather forecasts, the Farmers' Almanac was often used for *prognostication*."

Prone, supine – "Prone" means lying face down or having the palm down; having an inclination or tendency to something. "Supine" means lying face up or having the palm up; inactive due to indifference. "Patients are positioned *prone* for back surgery and *supine* for abdominal surgery."

Proportional, proportionate – Use "proportionate" when referring to two things in relationship to each other. "The output is *proportionate* to the energy expended." Use "proportional" to indicate there is a balance or correlation among a number of things. "The number of electoral districts is *proportional* to the area's population."

Protégé, prodigy – A "protégé" is a person whose career or welfare is promoted by a patron, usually an influential person. A "prodigy" is a person, especially a child or young person, with extraordinary talent or ability. "The opera conductor designed a new production to feature his *protégé*, a 14-year-old *prodigy* with a beautiful voice he intended to mold into a star soprano."

Prudent, cautious – Exercising good judgment or discretion is being "prudent" while specifically taking care to avoid risk or danger is being "cautious." "*Prudent* drivers obey all traffic laws." "*Cautious* joggers avoid Central Park after sunset."

Purposely, purposefully – "Purposely" means acting with a purpose in mind, deliberately. "Purposefully" describes a demeanor that exhibits a strong intention. "She *purposely* wore that dress to give an impression of confidence, and *purposefully* marched into the room to declare her candidacy."

Qualify, quantify – To "qualify" means to show some ability to perform in a particular capacity while to "quantify" refers to processing or calculating amounts. "I will *qualify* the candidate after I *quantify* the sales he has made."

Quite, quiet – "Quite" is an adverb meaning completely or very. "Quiet" means to be still, calm, silent. "The crowd became *quite quiet* after singing the national anthem."

Quixotic, chaotic – "Quixotic" means impulsive, unpredictable, caught up in the romance of noble deeds or pursuit of unreachable goals. "Chaotic" refers to a condition or place of disorder or confusion, a jumble. "The *chaotic* pile of articles strewn across her desk reflected a *quixotic* pursuit of her next crazy adventure."

Quotation, quote – A "quotation" is a set of words that is copied or repeated, such as a passage from a book, speech, etc. In commerce, it is also a statement of the market price of a commodity or security. A "quote" is a cost estimate from a vendor or service provider. Thus, you wouldn't write, "Here is a quote from Shakespeare." It should read, "Here is a quotation from Shakespeare" instead. However, some dictionaries and language experts state that "quote" as a noun is interchangeable with the first "quotation" definition above. The stricter usage that differentiates them is preferred but optional.

Rack, wrack – "Rack" is a framework with bars or shelves, also a medieval torture device. As a verb it means to strain or torment. "Wrack" refers to a wreck, damage, or destruction. "The stock market has been *wracked* by the recession as money managers *rack* their brains to make sense of it."

Raise, raze – "Raise" means to put up (e.g., raise a building). "Raze" means to level to the ground. "Years of toil went into *raising* the house that the tornado *razed* in moments."

Randy, raunchy – "Randy" means feeling great sexual desire, characterized by frank, uninhibited sexuality. "Raunchy" refers to vulgar or smutty, crude, earthy; also dirty, grimy, grubby. "The behavior of the novel's lead character changed from playfully *randy* to disgustingly *raunchy* when he moved into the mining town."

Rate, rank – "Rate" as a verb means to calculate the value of; to appraise. "Rank" as a verb means to take precedence over; to give a particular order or position to. "I'd *rate* that hotel 'five-star'; at least, it *ranks* at the top of the list of hotels I've ever stayed in."

Rational, rationale – "Rational" means having or exercising reason; based on reasoning or logic. "Rationale" means the fundamental reasons serving to account for something; explanation of reasons. "You are not being *rational*; your *rationale* for buying a car you can't afford is your passion for its red color."

Rationalize, justify – To "rationalize" is to ascribe actions to causes that seem reasonable but do not reflect the truth. To "justify" means to prove to be just, right, or reasonable. "I *rationalize* my desire to travel by finding a business reason to *justify* the cost."

Ravage, ravish – "Ravage" means to devastate; cause heavy damage. "Ravish" means to seize and carry away by force, physically or emotionally. "The tornado *ravaged* the countryside, leaving farmers *ravished* by the loss of the season's crops."

Reasoned, reasonable – "Reasoned" means to think logically while "reasonable" refers to sound thinking, being fair and within the bounds of common sense. "She *reasoned* that paying full price was a *reasonable* deal at this store."

Redress, address – "Redress" means to set right an unjust situation; to remedy or relieve; to adjust (a balance) evenly. "Address" means to speak to or give a speech to; to direct one's efforts towards; to deal with; to direct (a message) to the attention of; to mark with a destination. "In 1976 President Ford *addressed* the wrongful internment of Japanese during World War II; nearly 12 years later, President Reagan *redressed* the injustice through a Congressional act that awarded payments to surviving detainees."

Refuse, refuge, refuse – "Refuse" (pronounced re-FUSE, a verb) indicates an unwillingness to do, accept, give, or allow something. A "refuge" (REF-uge, a noun) is protection or shelter from danger or hardship. "Refuse" (REF-use, a noun) refers to items discarded or rejected as worthless; trash or rubbish. "Don't *refuse* him a place of *refuge*. Eating *refuse* from a dumpster is better than going hungry."

Regime, regimen – "Regime" refers to a period of rule and/or a governing body while "regimen" means a system of behavior or treatment. "Following a strict dietary *regimen* can feel like you're living in a military *regime*."

Rein, reign – A "rein" is a leather strap used by a rider or driver to control a horse or other animal; a means of restraint or guidance. "Reign" refers to the period during which a sovereign occupies a throne; rule or authority. "The police aim to *rein* in the insurgents so terror doesn't *reign* in the streets."

Renounce, denounce – "Renounce" means to give up, especially by formal declaration; to disown. "Denounce" means to condemn or censure openly or publicly; to accuse formally; to formally announce the ending of something (a treaty). "The young aristocrat *renounced* his title and *denounced* his family members for their refusal to sanction his relationship with a commoner."

Repel, repulse – "Repel" means to ward off, resist, reject, fight against. "Repulse" means to drive away, spurn, reject brusquely, cause feelings of disgust. These words can be used interchangeably, though "repulse" carries more emotion. "I *repel* your efforts to show me affection. You *repulse* me with your crude way of talking."

Repel, rappel – To "repel" is to drive back, resist, reject, produce a feeling of aversion. To "rappel" is to descend a steep incline by paying out a double rope that is attached at the top and wrapped around the body. "It's wise to wear clothes that *repel* water if you plan to *rappel* off that cliff near the waterfall."

Respectfully, respectively – "Respectfully" means to show politeness or deference. "Respectively" pertains to each of a number of persons. "The family members at the memorial service *respectfully* honored their dead father as they *respectively* (one-by-one) said a few words."

Restless, restive – "Restless" is being uneasy, agitated, in motion, while "restive" adds an element of stubbornness to an action or situation. "Under normal circumstances, the *restless* crowd would have dispersed but the insensitive politician elicited a *restive* response. The people wouldn't budge until he addressed their concerns."

Reticent, reluctant – "Reticent" means disposed to be silent or reserved while "reluctant" means hesitant or slow because of unwillingness. "She felt *reticent* (quiet) about sharing her opinions in front of others, while he felt *reluctant* (unwilling) to speak up because his ideas were unclear."

Retribution, retaliation – "Retribution" is something given or demanded in repayment, especially punishment. "Retaliation" is to return like for like in a negative context, i.e., evil for evil. "The court ordered payment as *retribution*, but that didn't satisfy those in the victim's family who wanted *retaliation* for the crime."

Revelation, revolution – "Revelation" refers to something realized or uncovered, especially a dramatic disclosure of something not previously understood. "Revolution" refers to the overthrow of one government and its replacement with another; a momentous change in a situation. It's also an orbital motion about a point (distinguished from axial rotation) as in planetary revolution about the sun. "It's been a *revelation* of the genius of humankind to witness today's *revolution* in computer technology."

Revere, revile – "Revere" means to regard with honor and respect, tinged with awe. "Revile" means to speak of or to abusively or with contempt. "George Washington is one of the most *revered* figures of the American Revolution while Benedict Arnold is one of the most *reviled*."

Review, revue – As both a noun and a verb, "review" refers to inspecting, surveying, or critically evaluating someone or something, such as a book, play, financial plan, life goal, work proposal, etc. "Revue," a noun, is a form of theatrical entertainment typically consisting of loosely connected and often satirical, skits, songs, and dances in which recent events and popular fads are parodied. "The entertainment editor was asked to write a *review* of the burlesque *revue*, but she was too shy to attend the performance."

Revolve, rotate – Both mean turn on or around an axis or a center. "Revolve" refers to recurring in cycles while "rotate" indicates alternating or taking turns. "A farmer's way of working *revolves* around the seasons." "Wise farmers *rotate* their crops periodically."

Right, rite – A "right" is something due to a person or governmental body by law, tradition, or nature; the interest possessed by law or custom in some intangible thing, i.e., movie rights. A "rite" is a prescribed or customary ritual for conducting a religious or other solemn ceremony; any customary observance or practice. "The First Amendment grants people the *right* to conduct *rites* in the religion of their choice."

Rigid, rigorous – "Rigid" implies uncompromising inflexibility, as in rigid rules of conduct. "Rigorous" suggests hardship and difficulty, as in rigorous training to become an Olympic athlete. "The team's *rigorous* goals required its members to follow a *rigid* practice schedule."

Ring, wring – A "ring" is a circular band of metal worn on the finger; a circular path or arrangement of things; an enclosure for certain sports and animal shows. To "ring" is to encircle. It also means to emit a sound like a bell being struck. To "wring" is to forcibly twist or compress, to extract by forceful effort, to clasp and twist (one's hands) in anguish. "As she attempted to *wring* out the wet towel, she noticed her wedding *ring* was gone."

Rise, raise – "Rise" means to get up or move from a low position to a high position. "Raise" means to lift an object or bring up something (e.g., raise children). "If you want your taxes to *rise*, please *raise* your hand."

Root, rout, route – As a verb, "root" means to pull, tear, or dig up by the roots, to remove completely (often followed by *up* or *out*). "We need a program to *root* out crime in our neighborhood." "Rout" (pronounced like shout) is an overwhelming victory or defeat. It also means to rummage or dig up (e.g., rout through the laundry). "Route" (pronounced either root or rout) refers to a course, way, or road. "The *route* to being in a championship is arduous while the event itself can either be a close game or a *rout.*"

S

Sadistic, seditious – "Sadistic" means deriving pleasure from cruelty, especially sexual gratification from inflicting pain. "Seditious" means relating to or guilty of engaging in treason (sedition), i.e., stirring up treasonous resistance to a government. "When it became evident the dictator was not merely harsh, but *sadistic*, the people became *seditious*."

Sallow, shallow – As an adjective "sallow" refers to a sickly yellowish hue or complexion. "Sallow" as a verb means to make that sallow color. The noun is a type of willow tree. As an adjective "shallow" means lacking physical depth; lacking depth of intellect, emotion, or knowledge; taking in a small amount of air in each inhalation. The verb means to make shallow. "To portray a character suffering from consumption, the actress used yellow makeup to appear *sallow* and she took rapid, *shallow* breaths."

Sardonic, sarcastic – While both refer to bitter, cutting, or derisive expression, "sardonic" goes beyond content to describe the manner of expression. "His *sarcastic* comment was delivered with a *sardonic* smile."

Secession, succession – "Secession" is the act of formally withdrawing from an alliance or association. When capitalized, it may refer to the withdrawal of 11 Southern states from the Union in 1860-61. "Succession" is the process of following in order or sequence. It can refer to the sequence in which one person succeeds another in office, estate, rank, or title. "The Supreme Court of Canada ruled that the *secession* of Quebec from Canada could not be brought about by popular vote." "The ailing monarch felt pressure to produce an heir and forestall fights that would erupt over *succession*."

Seize, cease – "Seize" means to grasp suddenly and forcibly; take or grab. "Cease" is to discontinue, put an end to something. "Before you *seize* a new opportunity, you may have to *cease* doing certain activities so you can plan your time."

Sensuous, sensual – "Sensuous" and "sensual" both mean perceived by, appealing to or gratifying the senses, but "sensuous" implies pure and aesthetic enjoyment (music, art), while "sensual" refers to satisfying bodily (especially sexual) appetites. "I enjoy the *sensuous* qualities of symphonies and Impressionist paintings. She prefers the *sensual* pleasures of scented oils and silk sheets."

Sentient, sentiment – "Sentient" is an adjective meaning to have sense perception, to be conscious. "Sentiment" is a noun referring to a thought, view, or attitude based on emotion rather than reason. "Some people believe *sentient* beings exist on other planets, while others consider that idea to be speculative *sentiment*."

Separate, disparate – As an adjective, "separate" means set or kept apart; disunited. "Disparate" means existing independently; fundamentally distinct in quality or kind. "Libraries usually have a *separate* section for reference books that cover a variety of *disparate* topics."

Setup, set up – The noun "setup" deals with a plan or arrangement. "The *setup* for the party includes entertainment and gourmet food." The two-word verb phrase "set up" means to arrange something. "We *set up* the entertain-ment for the party."

Sever, severe – To "sever" is to keep apart, cut, divide, or separate. "Severe" means unsparing, harsh, or strict. "Although she decided to *sever* their relationship, she didn't need to be so *severe* in her criticism of him."

Sew, sow – The verb "sew" (soh) means to join, fasten, or repair by stitching with a needle and thread or sewing machine. As a noun, "sow" (sou) refers to an adult female pig, especially one that has given birth; it can also refer to the adult female of other animals as well (e.g., bear). As a verb, "sow" (soh) means to plant seeds by scattering or to set something in motion (e.g., suspicion, an enterprise, etc.). "He wanted to *sew* a protective pouch for carrying the seeds he planned to *sow*."

Sheer, shear – As a verb, "sheer" means to swerve from a course; as an adjective, it means transparently thin; unmixed with anything else; utter; steep or almost vertical. To "shear" is to cut through something with a sharp instrument, espe-cially to cut or clip hair, fleece or wool; to travel through (air, water) as if by cutting. "There was a look of *sheer* terror in the eyes of the young sheep as the rancher approached, clippers in hand, to *shear* it."

Shutter, shudder – "Shutter" is either a cover for a window or the mechanism in a camera that controls the amount of light. To "shudder" is to vibrate, shake, or shiver. "I *shudder* to think the *shutter* on my camera might freeze at a crucial moment while taking photos."

Site, sight, cite – "Site" refers to a location (e.g., home *site*, web *site*) while "sight" refers to vision or seeing. "He was a *sight* for sore eyes." "Cite" means to quote or refer to a source. "You need to *cite* the creator of the original work."

Skilled, skillful – Both words show possession of a skill (a skillful athlete) but "skilled" is used in relation to a craftsman or technician (a skilled electrician). "To be a *skilled* contractor, he must be a *skillful* framer."

Small, less, fewer – When size is involved, use "small"; when importance is involved, use "less"; when quantity is involved, use "few" or "fewer." If you can count the number of items, use "fewer." "The *small* dog picked the *less* painful of two options. He faced *fewer* problems by running away than by attacking the porcupine."

Soar, sore – To "soar" means to fly upward like a bird or glide at a high altitude; to rise or ascend to a great height. "Sore" is an adjective that refers to something that either suffers from or causes physical or mental suffering; the noun refers to the cause of the pain, especially a painful spot on the body. "Although her legs were so *sore* that she wanted to collapse, her spirits *soared* with the thrill of accomplishment as she completed her first marathon."

Social, sociable – The adjective "social" describes a connection with a society, like a social club or a social ranking. "Sociable" means affable or friendly, as in sociable behavior. "Every *social* occasion requires people to be *sociable*."

Solve, resolve – "Solve" means to find a solution to a problem or puzzle. As a noun, "resolve" means to make a firm decision about or bring something to a successful conclusion. "Claire's teacher was encouraged by her pupil's *resolve* to stay after class and *solve* the puzzle."

Spectacle, spectacles – A "spectacle" is a large-scale public show or display. "Spectacles" are eyeglasses. "I attended the Hollywood premiere, but I couldn't fully appreciate the lavish *spectacle* because I forgot to bring my *spectacles*."

Spectacle, speculate – A "spectacle" is something, usually remarkable or impressive, that can be seen or viewed. "Speculate" means to reflect on a subject, often without conclusive evidence. "The *spectacle* at the collapsing circus tent led people to *speculate* about its cause."

Spurn, spur – To "spurn" means to reject with disdain or treat with contempt. To "spur" is to urge one's horse on with spurs; proceed hurriedly; to incite. "Being *spurned* by a girl who said she only dated athletes *spurred* him to lift weights and play football."

Stationary, stationery – "Stationery" is material for writing letters. "Stationary" is a fixed position. "I left my *stationery* (letter) in a car that wasn't *stationary* long enough for me to retrieve it." To help remember, the words "letter" and "stationery" both have an 'e'; the words "stay" and "stationary" both have an 'a.'

Strident, stringent – "Strident" means loud, harsh, or shrill in sound or quality. "Stringent" means strict or severe (as in rules); compelling or convincing (e.g., an argument), or tight (e.g., a money market). "The *stringent* library rules kept human voices to a whisper but couldn't stop the *strident* screeching of crows outside."

Stylus, stylist – A "stylus" is a sharp, pointed instrument used for writing, marking, or engraving. A "stylist" is a worker, designer or consultant in a field subject to changes in style, especially hairdressing, clothing, or interior decoration; a writer or speaker who cultivates an artful literary style. "The assistant used a *stylus* to enter information about the executive's appointment with a design *stylist*."

Suspicious, circumspect – To be "suspicious" is tending toward distrust. To be "circumspect" is to heed circumstances or consequences; to be prudent. "The more trusting of the two actors was *circumspect* about being in the audition, while the other was *suspicious* about how the final selection would be handled."

Swam, swum – To talk about the verb "swim" in the past tense, remember these examples: "Yesterday, I *swam* 20 laps (one time). I *have swum* that distance consistently (many times)." "Have" and "swum" belong together. It's incorrect to say, "I swum at the pool last week."

Sympathy, empathy – "Sympathy" is having pity or compassion for another's troubles without necessarily sharing their feelings. "Empathy" is putting yourself in another's place emotionally. "My *sympathy* goes out to those injured in the hurricane. I feel much *empathy* for those people I know personally."

Tack, tact – "Tack" as a verb or noun refers to taking a zig-zag course or abruptly changing direction or position. "Tact" refers to having a keen sense of what to say to avoid offending someone. "Use *tact* when talking to your prospective in-laws or you'll have to quickly *tack* to avoid their disapproving glares."

Tactful, tactical – "Tactful" means being or acting considerate or discreet. "Tactical" pertains to a plan or strategy for attaining a particular goal. "She was *tactful* enough to explain what was happening without giving away key *tactical* information."

Take, bring – Is the item you're talking about coming or going? If it is coming to a place, then someone "brings" it. If it's going somewhere, then someone "takes" it. "Will you *bring* me a glass of water, please?" "Yes I will, after I *take* the dirty glasses away."

Team, teem – "Team" or "team up" means to bring people together to form a team. "Teem" means to abound or swarm with activity. "The playing fields *teem* with excitement every time the players *team* up to play soccer."

Tenet, tenant – "Tenet" refers to an opinion, principle, dogma, belief, or doctrine that a person holds true (sometimes spelled tenent). "Tenant" is a person or group who occupies property owned by another for a period of time; a lessee. "The central *tenet* of being a squatter is never to pay rent as a *tenant.*"

Tepid, torpid – "Tepid" pertains to a moderately warm or lukewarm liquid; lacking in emotional warmth or enthusiasm; halfhearted. "Torpid" means having lost the power of exertion and feeling; numb; dormant; dull or sluggish. "His *tepid* mood didn't endear him to his co-workers, but his *torpid* attitude made him especially difficult to work with."

Testimony, testimonial – A "testimony" is a declaration or affirmation of fact, such as given before a court. A "testimonial" is a formal or written statement affirming a truth. "The strong *testimony* he gave in court could be regarded as a *testimonial* to her strong character."

That, which – Use "that" when the following phrase is essential to the meaning of the sentence. "We provide guides *that* serve as an alternative to our programs." Use "which" when the phrase gives information but isn't critical to understanding the sentence. "The self-teaching guides, *which* complement services we offer, provide an alternative to our programs." "Those guides *that* complement the services we offer should be printed."

That, who – "That" relates to things while "who" relates to people. "I have a friend *who* did me a favor, one *that* I greatly appreciated."

Their, there, they're – "Their" (possessive pronoun) indicates possession. "It is *their* wish." "There" (adverb) refers to a location or place. "*There* is a place for us." "They're" (contraction) means "they are" – the apostrophe takes the place of the missing letter. "*They're* coming over for a drink."

Then, than – "Then" means soon after or at that time while "than" sets up a comparison. "Let's eat, *then* go shopping." "He's shorter *than* his brother."

Toe the line, tow the line – The idiom "toe the line" comes from a foot-racing rule requiring competitors to keep their feet behind a "line" or on a "mark" at the start of a race. Spelling "toe" as "tow" is incorrect given this meaning.

Tolerant, tolerable – "Tolerant" means inclined to tolerate, particularly the beliefs or behavior of others; able to endure adverse environmental conditions (e.g., a drought-tolerant plant). "Tolerable" means capable of being tolerated; moderately good; passable. "She was *tolerant* of her toddler's picky eating habits, but still hoped he would outgrow his belief that no food was *tolerable* without adding ketchup."

Tortuous, torturous – Although both words come from the Latin "torqure" (to twist, wind, wrench), "tortuous" refers to something that's winding or crooked while "torturous" means painfully unpleasant. "The *tortuous* mountain road can be *torturous* if you have to ride up that road on a bicycle."

Track, tract – As a noun, "track" can be any evidence of something that has passed, such as the wake of a ship or a pattern of footprints. It is also the wheel-to-wheel width of a vehicle and an element of the sport of track and field. As a verb, "track" means to trace, follow or search for, or travel over. "Tract," a noun, is an extent or lapse of time as well as a stretch of land. It can also be a leaflet of propaganda or a system of body parts that act together to perform a function, such as the digestive tract. "My outdoor model railroad *track* is laid on a *tract* in our back yard."

Transparent, translucent – When an object is "transparent" it is completely see-through. With a "translucent" object, light goes through it but you can't see to the other side. "We can see the view clearly through the *transparent* window in the kitchen but not through the *translucent* glass in the bathroom."

Treaty, treatise – "Treaty" means a formal agreement between states or governments. "Treatise" is a formal exposition in writing about a subject. It's longer and more detailed than an essay. "Researchers have written *treatise* after treatise examining events that led to the signing of the peace *treaty*."

Tremulous, tremendous – "Tremulous" means characterized by trembling, as from fear, nervousness, or weakness; timid or fearful. "Tremendous" means extraordinarily great in size, amount, or intensity; exciting fear or trembling through its terrifying magnitude. "The shy child began to recite her lines in a *tremulous* voice, but when the first act of the school play received *tremendous* applause, her delivery became more confident."

Trooper, trouper – A "trooper" is a police officer, cavalry soldier, or horse. A "trouper" is a loyal, uncomplaining, hard-working person; a member of a theatrical company or a veteran actor. "The *trooper* was parked just over the hill with a radar gun." "He's been with the company through thick and thin, a real *trouper*."

Turbid, torpid – "Turbid" means containing stirred up sediment or particles, dense (such as smoke or fog), or muddled. "Torpid" means sluggish, lethargic, apathetic, or dormant (such as a hibernating animal). "The *turbid* water where waves crashed against the reef hid the *torpid* sea turtle until it surfaced to breathe."

Unconscious, subconscious – "Unconscious" means without awareness, sensation, or cognition; not perceived at the level of awareness; without conscious volition or intent. "Subconscious" means imperfectly or not wholly conscious; occurring just below the level of consciousness. "To a psychoanalyst, an *unconscious* gesture can help reveal *subconscious* motivations."

Undo, undue – To "undo" is to reverse the doing of, to open or unfasten, or to bring to ruin. "Undue" means excessive, unjustifiable, improper; not yet payable. "If you *undo* my buttons with *undue* haste, they will pop off!"

Urban, urbane – "Urban" means relating to, characteristic of, or located in a city. "Urbane" means elegant, refined, and sophisticated in manner. "She moved from a small, *urban* apartment to an estate in the countryside after marrying the handsome, *urbane* aristocrat."

Verbalize, vocalize – "Verbalize" means to express something in words (whether by speaking, writing, sign language, or other means). "Vocalize" refers to producing sounds using the voice. "It takes skill and practice to *verbalize* messages through sign language to a hearing-impaired audience while simultaneously *vocalizing* for attendees who can hear."

Verbiage, verbage *(not a real word)* – These are often confused, yet only "verbiage" is a legitimate word in proper English. "Verbiage" means the manner in which something is expressed verbally; an excess of words. "The editor's job is to prune *verbiage* from a fledgling writer's overwritten text." In contrast, "verbage" can be used as jargon that is more derogatory than "verbiage."

Vial, vile – A "vial" is a small container, while "vile" is a term used for something unpleasant, disgusting, and morally reprehensible. "A spilled *vial* of blood is regarded as interesting by some and completely *vile* by others."

Voluble, volatile – "Voluble" is characterized by a ready flow of speech. "Volatile" means tending to break out into violence, liable to sharp or sudden changes. "Two glasses of wine made him *voluble* and three made him downright nasty and *volatile*."

Voracious, vicious – "Voracious" means having an insatiable appetite. "Vicious" means characterized by violent or destructive behavior. "*Voracious* viewers of action movies are more likely to mimic the *vicious* behavior they see on screen than those who don't."

Waver, waiver – "Waver" (verb) means to move unsteadily back and forth; to show indecision; to falter; to tremble or quaver in sound; to flicker or glimmer in light. "Waiver" is an intentional relinquishment of a right, claim, or privilege (also the document that evidences such relinquishment). "The officials didn't *waver* in their decision about accepting any liability for injuries. They made the athlete sign a *waiver* of responsibility before allowing her to compete."

Wave, waive – "Wave" (verb) means to move freely, gently back and forth or up and down, as by the action of air currents, sea swells, etc. To "waive" (verb) is to refrain from claiming or insisting on something, to give up, forgo. "With cameras showing the courthouse flags *waving* in the background, the accused robber told TV reporters he would *waive* his right to be represented by a lawyer."

Weary, wary – "Weary" means to be physically or mentally tired due to hard work, exertion or strain. It also means to be impatient or dissatisfied with something (e.g., weary of excuses). "Wary" is being watchful or on guard against danger. "Even if you become *weary* while driving, being *wary* of the traffic around you should be first priority."

Whale, wail – A "whale" is a marine mammal with a fishlike body, flippers, horizontal tail flukes, and a blowhole. "Wail" means to utter a prolonged, usually high-pitched, inarticulate, mournful cry; to grieve or protest loudly and bitterly. As a noun, it's a long, loud, high-pitched sound. "In the excitement of seeing a *whale* breach, the child dropped his favorite toy overboard and began to *wail*."

Wheedle, whittle – "Wheedle" means to entice by soft words or flattery; to coax; to gain by flattery or guile. "Whittle" means to cut small bits or pare shavings (e.g., from a piece of wood). It also refers to reducing gradually, as if by whittling with a knife. "The unknown pair *wheedled* their way into a holiday party and *whittled* away at every dessert on the table."

Where, when, in which – Think carefully about the exact meaning of your sentence when selecting the right bridge words. Use "where" for place or location; "when" for time; "in which" for things. "They decided *when* (not where) the teenager had to start paying rent to his parents." "I examined a case *in which* (not where) opportunities for improvement exist." "He's not sure *where* he put his glasses."

Who, whom – Use "who" as the subject of a sentence or clause. Use "whom" as an object. Think of "who" as an equivalent for the personal pronouns he, she, or they, while "whom" is similar to him, her, or them. "*Whom* did you select for the presentation?" (You selected him/her/them.) "*Who* will be selected?" (He/she/they will be selected.)

Who's, whose – "Who's" is a contraction for "who is" or "who has". "Whose" shows ownership. "*Who's* responsible for correcting this error? *Whose* mistake is it anyway?"

Wiggle, wriggle – "Wiggle" as a verb means to move or go with short, quick, irregular movements from side to side. As a noun, wiggle is a movement. "Wriggle" means to twist to and fro; writhe; squirm like a snake; to make one's way by shifts or expedients (often followed by out). "To *wriggle* out of washing the dishes, he *wiggled* a candy in front of his sister as an enticement to clean them."

Winery, vineyard – "Winery" is a place for making wine. "Vineyard" is a farm of grapevines where wine grapes are produced. "Often, a *winery* is built right next to the *vineyard* where the grapes are grown."

Worthy, worthwhile – "Worthy" means having adequate or great merit, character, or value; deserving. "Worthwhile" refers to an activity that repays one's time, attention, interest, work, trouble. "To make your time *worthwhile*, it's best to commit to a cause that's *worthy* and deserving of the effort required." ("Worthwhile" is sometimes used as a synonym for "worthy.")

Wreck, wreak – "Wreck" means to cause the ruin or destruction of something; a vessel, structure; a person in a state of ruin or dilapidation. "Wreak" means to inflict, execute, or bring about vengeance, punishment, havoc; to express anger, malevolence, or resentment. "Many boats were *wrecked* as the hurricane *wreaked* havoc along the coast."

Your, you're – "Your" shows possession; "you're" is a contraction that means "you are." "When *your* ship comes in, *you're* a wealthy person."

ABOUT THE CREATOR OF
WORD TRIPPERS

BARBARA MCNICHOL

As an editor of nonfiction books and articles, Barbara absolutely loves what she does because of the fabulous people she works with: successful professionals who share their passion through speaking, writing, and marketing. In particular, she enjoys collaborating with inspired, giving people who deliver powerful messages that make a difference in our world. If that's you, allow Barbara to add power to your pen through her editorial services.

For details about Barbara McNichol Editorial services, visit **www.BarbaraMcNichol.com** or call **877-696-4899**.

Email: Editor@BarbaraMcNichol.com

Blog: www.NonfictionBookEditor.com

Member: National Speakers Association (NSA)
Global Speakers Federation (GSF)
National Association for Independent Writers and Editors (NAIWE)

Word Tripper of the Week e-newsletter

Keep those Trippers coming! Bring regular reminders about using the right word in the right way into your inbox.

Sign up at **www.WordTrippers.com.**

Add Power to Your Pen e-newsletter

Receive valuable insights every month on how to strengthen your writing, whatever your purpose.

Sign up at **www.BarbaraMcNichol.com.**

Nonfictionbookeditor.com blog

Find a wealth of tips, techniques, and resources for writing your nonfiction books and articles.

Visit **www.nonfictionbookeditor.com.**

BARBARA MCNICHOL EDITORIAL

EDITING NONFICTION BOOKS, PROPOSALS, ARTICLES, AND MARKETING MATERIALS FOR AUTHORS, SPEAKERS, AND ENTREPRENEURS.

PRAISE FOR *WORD TRIPPERS*
FROM FANS OF "WORD TRIPPER OF THE WEEK"

"Word Trippers are concise and down to earth: nothing snobby about Barbara McNichol's approach to clear thinking and lively writing. Whether you write for a living or just want to write correctly, Word Trippers is a handy resource."

> ~ George Mason, faithful subscriber

"I highly recommend Word Trippers—a delightful and quite useful reference with great information from a world class book editor, Barbara McNichol."

> ~ Anita Paul, speaker, former court reporter

"Word Trippers! As a writer and speaker, words are right up there with chocolate for me! There's something scintillating in capturing the precise expression to convey my message. And there's nothing more pedestrian than seeing the wrong use of a common word. For those who worship words like I do, you'll fall in love with Barbara McNichol's Word Trippers book. An avid student of language, she will make sure you never have foot-in-mouth disease again!"

> ~ Karen Wright, speaker, author

"It's too easy to let word skills slip and become rusty or obsolete. Word Trippers is a quick and easy way to maintain word usage skills."

> ~ Jill Easterday, speaker, author

"I enjoy your mailings and appreciate your succinct descriptions of the language distinctions."

> ~ Jan Carothers, CPC, speaker, author

"At the National Speakers Association conventions, writer and editor Barbara McNichol is a sparkling, understated presence. I've watched firsthand as she helps people clarify and shape their messages, and her Word Trippers ebook is the best I've seen on the topic."

~ Kare Anderson, author, speaker

"This time you really hit home. I thought my grammar was good, but I frequently misuse 'hopefully' and maybe even the other three. I was shocked!"

~ Lynn Murphy, speaker, author

"It's like a cleansing, reading your correct use of English! I feel purified. Refreshed. Validated."

~ Rosalyn Kirkel, speaker, author

"I recently presented a seminar and checked Word Trippers several times to make sure I had the correct word and spelling. You've helped raise my awareness!"

~ Geri Markel, speaker, author

"You've defined my pet peeve with eager and anxious!"
~ Michelle Cubas, speaker, author

"I find your grammer, grimmer, grammar updates helpful. (And you know I need the help.)"

~ Brian O'Malley, speaker, author

"I greatly enjoy your Word Tripper newsletter and really appreciate all the work that goes into it. I share your passion for English, spelling, and grammar, and even after 22 years in my field, I'm still learning new things!"

~ Deanna Dean, court reporter

"I want to say how much I enjoy your newsletter. Just the right length, and always meaty. I am convinced this is important, and I am persuaded to do my part to respect the English language."

~ Sheila Feigelson, author, speaker

"I thoroughly enjoy your weekly Word Trippers. They are informative and beneficial for those who are interested in mastering the English language."

~ Nathanael Mayhew, faithful subscriber

"I always enjoy seeing your name in my mailbox, knowing you will have brought me another useful word tool."

~ Hazel Harris, faithful subscriber

"I always find your word trippers educational and helpful. Peace and Harmony."

~ Agnes Paulsen, choir director

"I love to see our language used properly. Your notes give me hope that lots of other people love to see that, too."

~ Chas Ridley, writer

"The 'usage-based' changes in our grammar (not grammer) lead to interesting turns of phrase."

~ Marie Davis, faithful subscriber

"Your Word Trippers are invaluable. I have a 13-year-old granddaughter I'll share them with."

~ Ben Leichling, speaker

"It makes me crazy when our language is abused and degraded. Word Trippers should be required reading for every student!"

~ Diane Kinared, faithful subscriber

"Keep providing us with such wonderful information. Hats off to you."

~ Ali Ammar, faithful subscriber

"I love your WordTrippers. Helps me greatly in my effort not to trip over my own words."

~ Raleigh Pinskey, author, speaker

"When I was trying to figure out whether to use 'passed' or 'past'. The MS Bookshelf definition still wasn't clear enough – your Word Trippers guide was easier to understand."

~ Mary Marcdante, author, speaker

"I'd like to give readers some quotes from your booklet (and, of course, credit you) and recommend they subscribe to your monthly e-mail newsletter, as I do."

~ Mona Scott James (aka Mrs. Bluezette)

"Your Word Trippers piece is always my favorite. Thanks."

~ George R. Walther, CSP, CPAE, author, speaker

"I just love your Word Trippers. Your excellent tips and gentle reminders to use our language appropriately is such good mental gymnastics."

~ Susanne Jalbert, businesswoman

"... all the nuns who tried to teach me rally around above me singing hallelujah . . . Keep up the good work. So many English teachers will have you recognized as a saint."

~ a Catholic fan, Joni Seivert, consultant

"When I switched jobs, yours was one of the few writing news-letters I kept due to the useful tips I can immediately employ."

~ Charlotte Pack, subscriber

"Great ezine/tips this month. Thanks."

~ Dan Poynter, author, speaker, self-publishing guru
(Thanks to Dan who features Word Trippers in his excellent ezine for self-published authors, "Publishing Poynters," at www.parapub.com)

SIGN UP TODAY FOR YOUR OWN WORD TRIPPER OF THE WEEK!
WWW.WORDTRIPPERS.COM